The Art of
DANCE
In Education

The Art of
DANCE
In Education

Jacqueline M. Smith-Autard

A & C Black · London

First Published 1994

A & C Black (Publishers) Limited
35 Bedford Row, London WC1R 4JH

ISBN 0–7136–3897–4

A CIP Catalogue record for this book is available from the British Library.

Typeset in Linotron 10 on 12pt Palatino by Florencetype Ltd, Kewstoke, Avon
Printed and bound in Great Britain by Biddles Ltd, Guildford, Surrey

Contents

ACKNOWLEDGEMENTS

I thank the students and staff of Bedford College of Higher Education (De Montfort University), particularly Sarah Stevens and Brigitte Boast, for their contribution to the development of new dance modules in the BA Hons. modular degree course which commenced in 1990. These modules are discussed as examples of the art of dance in higher education in Chapter 4 of this book.

I am also indebted to Sarah Stevens for the many hours of lively debate on concepts discussed in this book and to my partner for his support and abundant patience in reading the text.

Preface

The aim of this book is to present a theoretical basis for the art of dance in education and to demonstrate how it applies to current practice. To date, there is no one text which provides a theoretical framework to support it. This text fills the gap in offering teachers a thoroughly-argued rationale and a means of developing a clearer understanding of what and how to teach the art of dance in education. It is **not** concerned with other types of dance, e.g. social or folk dance, and their role in education.

The focus in this book is on dance in schools, colleges and universities (state or private) which offer full-time education and form part of the national provision for compulsory education between the ages of five and sixteen, or for further and higher education for those wishing to continue. (The book is also relevant to adult education where this provides the content offered in full-time education.)

There is no attempt to discuss the part-time opportunities for dance experiences offered by dance schools, clubs, youth groups or even by extra-curricular dance activities at the above-mentioned schools and colleges. Vocational schools are also excluded, even those offering full-time education, because they do not normally offer the *curriculum* art of dance experience that is under scrutiny here. The focus is, therefore, on schools, colleges and universities, and on what occurs in the name of dance within curriculum time.

This book has been in process for a number of years. The foundational premise that the art of dance in education is best considered as a *midway* model combining the best practices of two opposing models was first proposed in my master's dissertation (1977). This view developed out of the initial exploration of the concept of dance as art discussed in *Dance Composition* (1976) in which the three-stranded process of creating, performing and appreciating dances was identified. In several subsequent articles and reports of conference proceedings*, these ideas were developed and extended, much informed by the practical experience of teaching dance across the primary, secondary and higher education sectors.

* Smith, J.M., 'Dance as Art Education: new directions in young people dancing' in the proceedings of a conference, *Dance and the Child International*, Volume 1: *Dance Education*, 1988. This paper and a subsequent paper for the same agency in 1990 form the basis of chapter 1.

Introduction

Dance is a broad term which covers many varied activities and dance is performed for many reasons. The need here is to make clear what the term *art of dance* has come to mean in dance education parlance over the past thirty years. This period has seen significant changes in dance in education. An outline of these changes has been written elsewhere* and chapter 1 summarises the essential details for the purpose of this text.

The term *art* is much debated in philosophical treatises. Here the concern is not with the meaning of art as a concept but with the meaning that the word has when it prefaces or follows the term *dance*. In education the *art of dance* or, perhaps more commonly, *dance as art* has been a label used to distinguish content and teaching approaches which are different from those associated with former terms such as *modern educational dance, creative dance* or *expressive dance*.

Changes in recent years have made it helpful to use the qualifying noun of *art* with *dance*. Dance as art shares the characteristics of other forms of art such as painting, poetry, music and drama. It puts dance alongside other arts in the production of objects for aesthetic enjoyment. This is, of course, not the only function of art works but it is an important and distinguishing one. It also brings into focus the processes of creating, performing and appreciating. Indeed, in education these processes are key factors in determining teaching and learning programmes. Even the youngest pupils can engage in creating, performing and appreciating dances. Dance art works are not only publicly acknowledged professional performances but also the dances that children make for themselves.

* *Dance Composition*, second edition, Jacqueline Smith-Autard, 1992

1

In education, then, the art of dance is centrally concerned with the creating, performing and appreciating of art works which cannot be produced in a vacuum. As in other arts, reference is made to publicly-recognised examples of dance works of which pupils must be aware. This requires some contact with the professional world of dance which was ignored in former school or college dance education practice.

Chapter 1 defines and analyses the *midway* art of dance in education model examining the features that it has retained from other models and those that are new and distinctive. This analysis exposes the underlying theory of the art of dance in education.

Chapters 2 and 3 apply the theoretical framework to teaching and learning dance in primary and secondary education. In both these chapters one example of a dance outcome is scrutinised in relation to the *midway* model and to the programmes of study for dance in key stages 1, 2, 3 and 4 of the National Curriculum.

Chapter 4 applies to higher education the theoretical framework underpinning the *midway* model. In this context, a range of dance modules offered as part of the modular BA Hons degree course in one institution is examined. Since a number of modules are discussed in this chapter, no further examples are included in the appendix.

The appendix contains a full interpretation of the content in programmes of study for key stages 1 to 4. It also includes the content of lessons leading to the dance outcomes analysed in chapters 2 and 3. Further examples of work suitable for the primary and secondary age range provide more ideas for practice.

1

The Art of Dance in Education – A Theoretical Basis

Models for teaching should always be dynamic and constantly changing, so to define and promote any one model for teaching may seem over-prescriptive.

Processes of change, however, often occur in practice well before any model can be defined, and indeed, new practice has to develop before it is possible to reflect on its nature. When the new practice has been tried and tested by teachers and students it becomes necessary to define and promulgate the practice and theories which underpin it in order that it becomes known and developed as a valued model for teaching. The model then becomes reinforced through initial teacher training, in-service courses and texts for teachers, so disseminating and developing its aims, content, methodologies and processes of assessment.

The dominant model for dance education today has been labelled the *dance as art* model (in this book it is called the *art of dance* model). This is the model which I proposed in 1976 in my book *Dance Composition* and which was strongly advocated in the subsequent Calouste Gulbenkian Foundation report *Dance Education and Training in Britain* (1980). It is also the model implicit in the statutory programmes of study for dance within the DES *Physical Education in the National Curriculum* 1992 order and GCSE, AS and A level syllabuses. The *art of dance* model seems thus to have been confirmed as a model of 'good practice' to which all school pupils are entitled at least at key stages 1 and 2 where dance is a compulsory part of the physical education programme.

As we have seen, the *art of dance* model did not emerge suddenly – it has taken at least fifteen years to develop. One of the first dance theoreticians to propose it was Betty Redfern (1972), but the content

3

and methods of teaching emerged gradually and have been the main focus of my work since 1965. The theoretical basis of the art of dance model presented below is the result of my reflection on the nature of current practice in dance education and is grounded in much experience of different approaches. Although it has new and unique features of its own, it has retained elements of the two models which preceded it. For this reason, although the old elements are reoriented, it can be called a *midway* model.

Predecessors of the art of dance model

The somewhat 'free', 'open' and 'child-centred' approach which has been variously labelled *modern educational dance, creative dance,* and the like, was derived from Rudolf Laban's ideas in the late 1940s and lasted as the consensus practice until the early 1970s. The essential characteristic of his 'educational' model was its emphasis on the *process of dancing and its affective/experiential contribution to the participant's overall development as a moving/feeling being.* The benefits of feeling personal expressive significance in movement outcomes derived from various stimuli were considered important contributions to the all-round development of the personality. Here, emphasis was laid equally on the physical, emotional and social dimensions of the personality, the development of which might be fostered in dance movement situations in which spontaneous individual responses were complemented by group work where interaction through movement was the aim. In particular, the stress was on a meaningful *process* rather than on the outcome or *product* which might emerge.

The opposing model which influenced much of what was going on in dance education in secondary schools, further and higher education colleges in the 1960s and 1970s, could be called the *professional* model in that the main aim was to produce highly skilled dancers and theatrically defined dance products for presentation to audiences. Such dance outcomes would be considered as vehicles through which the range of dance skills constituting any one style could be exhibited. The content of such courses was an already-defined set of dance skills in the style of dance being studied, e.g. Graham, Cunningham, ballet or jazz. If time allowed, the prescribed formulae for choreography as laid down by American contemporary dance teachers such as Humphrey and H'Doubler were also included. This very particular approach was apparent until the late 1970s in *some* quarters of dance education (though the majority of school teachers, especially primary teachers, still held to the Laban *educational* model). Of course, there was much criticism of those who adopted the *professional* training model especially since the prescribed techniques needed time spent on body training leaving no time for creative work in the short periods of dance allowed in secondary schools. This *product-based* model is that which is used fully and expertly by our professional dance training schools and colleges where the aim is to produce dancers as performers. Such a form of dance education is surely not suited to the majority.

A **MIDWAY** *MODEL*

Today's *midway* model amalgamates some of the elements of the *educational* and *professional* models, yet includes new ideas, too. Its distinctiveness lies in the concept of the art of dance in education contributing towards artistic education, aesthetic education and cultural education. It identifies the three strands of creating, performing and appreciating dances as the conceptual basis under-lying dance experiences for pupils. The need for balance between creating, performing and viewing dances, on the one hand, and an overall concern, on the other, that pupils come to appreciate dances (their own and those produced professionally) as art works, has become the central organising principle of dance education in the 1990s.

In order that we understand why, for me, the model is labelled the *midway* model, a list of features which, to a lesser or greater degree, it retains from its predecessors is presented below. This is followed by discussion of each of them and the modification or reorientation that has occurred because of the changes in the conceptual basis for the art of dance in education. Central themes of each of the past models have been listed and the ensuing discussion demonstrates how the art of dance model has laid equal emphasis on these previously opposing concepts.

Table of features retained from the **educational** and **professional** models

EDUCATIONAL MODEL	PROFESSIONAL MODEL
Emphasis on the process	Emphasis on the product
Emphasis on development of creativity, imagination and individuality	Emphasis on knowledge of theatre dance as the model towards which to aspire
Emphasis on feelings – subjectivity of experience	Emphasis on objective ends – e.g. trained bodies for performance of dances
Emphasis on a set of principles as a source of content	Emphasis on stylistically-defined dance techniques as content
Emphasis on a problem-solving approach to teaching – teacher as guide, pupil as agent in own learning	Emphasis on directed teaching – teacher as expert, pupil as apprentice.

Process versus product

Emphasis on process

The *educational* dance model was often regarded as an instrumental means of permitting the expression of the individual's personality in the process of dancing. Attention was paid to the subjective experience of creating and expressing during the act of dancing rather than to the object created. The object, if there was one as outcome of the dance experience, was judged more in terms of personal gains, for example, sense of satisfaction, release of emotions, feelings of joy. Laban's emphasis on process as an important feature of dance education encompasses elements of a romantic ideology, with dance seen as a means through which the individual may become aware of him/herself, develop creative/expressive abilities and social skills in group work. This makes the process of creating and performing dance totally subjective and, as Best (1985) states, 'impossible to assess and educate'. Best goes on to argue that mental processes involved in creative work which cannot be seen cannot be judged except through the end products. Similarly, in the context of performance, no matter how wonderful the process feels to the performer, there is surely concern for what is produced in terms of aesthetic and artistic appeal.

The view that it is process alone that counts and that the product is immaterial cannot be considered viable, especially in the current educational climate which emphasises evaluation, assessment of attainment and teacher accountability. Indeed, to place importance on an intangible and immeasurable process would have put dance into a vulnerable position within the National Curriculum in which achievement in terms of skills, knowledge and understanding is paramount.

The quality of the process then should be reflected in the quality of the product. This means that the process skills of creativity, for example, can only be judged as indicative of originality, flexibility, flair or inventiveness, if the product has signs of these qualities. Such a judgement is to be made in relation to other products generated by the individual, by peers or by artists of recognised status in the public world, whichever is the most appropriate. Similarly, the process skills of performance such as focus, characterisation, projection of meaning and artistry cannot be assessed without reference to shared knowledge of such criteria.

Emphasis on product

As indicated above, the central idea underlying the use of the *professional* model in secondary schools and colleges in the 1960s and 1970s, was that adolescents and young adults were ready and had a need for the development of technical skills. Teachers in Britain adopted this model primarily because the *educational* model had no identifiable skill repertoire. Their aims, it appeared, were to secure motivation and enjoyment of dance through the professional aura of technical classes, students identifying such work with theatrical dance, which was becoming more and more accessible through television, theatre and visits of artists in schools. It was believed that by this means the dance experience would become more relevant because the ends, even if unattainable for most, were identifiable.

To achieve a theatrically-styled and skilled performance level was the emphasised product of the *professional* model. This was the main aim even if other goals, such as development of imaginative and creative responses, were not met. The emphasis on skilled bodily performance in most cases required concentration on one technique only in the time available. This meant that if, for example, the Graham technique was the medium, the students might become very skilled and knowledgeable in this small part but would remain ignorant of dance as a richly diversified whole. This constituted a very narrow dance experience which could hardly be called dance education. In this way, the *professional* model, especially in the hands of inexperienced teachers, became devoid of process in that pupils only received and practised prescribed skills and dances. No good dance teacher would limit pupils to this form of training. Such indoctrination became taboo even in examination programmes in which pre-set dances had to be learned and performed. Rather, the view promoted here is that personally textured and artistic rendering of such examination pieces, like music, is much the favoured presentation.

Equal emphasis on process and on product

Clearly then, the art of dance in education model should emphasise neither process or product in the ways in which the preceding *educational* and *professional* models seemed to advocate. Rather, there should be equal emphasis on both quality of process and quality of product. The means towards this will be discussed in depth later in the book, but suffice it to say that, in the creating of dances for example, the process of exploration, selection and final refinement can be as rich and as personalised as the teacher deems suitable for the experience of the pupils and their abilities to handle the dance tasks given. First, however, there must be some clear objectives on the nature of the product to be devised and, again in the words of Best (1985), 'in order to produce it one needs to have learned the requisite discipline of the medium of expression'.

Moreover, in performing dances or dance studies the process of coming to know the nuances of expression and meaning intrinsic to the content and form of the piece is vitally important if the performance is to have 'life' and feeling in its presentation. Too often, as a GCSE or A level examiner one is confronted with a mechanically sound but lifeless rendition of a technical dance study. Usually this indicates the way it has been taught. If the technique involved has been mastered by the pupil, then, as with an actor who has learned his words, much more is required in the performance of the product. In the art of dance model, there is much to be learned through the process and about the product in creating and performing dances.

Creativity, imagination and individuality versus acquisition of knowledge of theatre dance

Emphasis on creativity, imagination and individuality

In the words of Haynes in Abbs (1987), it appears that Laban:

> viewed the dancer as creator ... and placed strong emphasis on personal expression; on spontaneous improvisation and experimentation; on creative activity as a means of evolving a style of dance which was 'true' to the individual personality. One of the fundamental aims of his work was embodied in the belief that a training in the 'art of movement' facilitated harmonisation of the individual and helped lead towards self realisation (towards what Jung called the process of individualisation).

Hence, development of creativity, imagination and individuality through making personal responses to the given tasks in dance were the stated concerns of the *educational* model. However, recent writings of eminent philosophers such as Best demonstrate just how misconceived were these notions. They dispute that such development could occur in the context of exploring and experiencing movement for oneself and that creativity and imagination are inborn facilities which need not be educated. As Best (1985) says:

> To be creative requires a grasp of the criteria of validity and value in the activity in question. Originality is given its sense only against a background of the traditional ... imagination is imagination only in so far as it operates within limits.

What are these criteria of validity? What is the background of the traditional in dance education? What are the limits placed upon the imagination?

The answers must lie in the fact that the art of dance, like other art forms, is a public phenomenon which is removed from the everyday into the 'art world'. It is, therefore, subject to the influence of public conventions, styles and meanings; pupils learning to 'create' in dance (including those at primary stage) need to learn how to portray or discern meaning in dance movement and at the same time become aware of and use the shared public references. The means to this end will be discussed later, but here it is important to acknowledge that creating in dance is not going to advance beyond the cathartic release of personal feelings through unstructured and self-expressive movement responses unless teachers understand how creativity and imagination *can* be educated. This recognition does not prevent the individual's feelings and ideas from entering the expressive form. Although it is not easy to say how this happens, it is often the case that pupils who have studied dance choreography within the theatre as part of their GCSE course, for example, nevertheless produce dances which are fresh, original and obviously derived from their own experiences.

Clearly then, dance in education should no longer be a rarefied and differentiated activity. Rather, as indicated previously, creating and imagining in the dance context *depend* upon extending from the givens towards something new. As in other arts, there is need for constant reference to and interaction with the art of dance as it exists in the public world.

Emphasis on knowledge of theatre dance

From the above, it would appear that the *professional* model holds the answer for the art of dance in education in that there is constant reference to the public theatrical art model. However, to adopt the same content and procedures normally associated with training performers and choreographers in the professional context is not recommended either. Such training requires full-time courses containing daily classes in techniques which require certain mastery levels prior to the learning and practising of repertoire. Some courses also study the art of choreography based mostly on prescribed formulae to be learned and employed. This sort of programme (though much modified and developed) will be discussed in the context of further and higher education later in the book but, at school level, there is no time for this intensive and professionally-oriented training. As suggested earlier, for those who adopted this model there was a tendency to restrict the content to study and practice of the technique aspect of the theatre dance model. Dance in education must be more embracing and less predetermined in terms of its outcomes than the making of professional dancers and choreographers.

The main emphasis must be placed on developing the pupils' knowledge of the many dimensions of the art of dance. Thus the type and range of study differ from those outlined in the *professional* model with its dominant focus on technique as a prerequisite to artistic participation. Its essential differences lie in the equality of emphasis put on the three strands (creating, performing and viewing dances) even for beginners and in the concept of the art of dance as a publicly-derived phenomenon.

In the study of creating dances, for example, pupils should become aware of the styles and choreographic conventions which characterise the range of works available to them in the theatre repertory. These, like musical compositions, are historically and socially derived and extend from those termed classical ballet to those of 'new dance' categorisation. Knowledge of this variety, which should grow slowly through the school years, provides students with a rich source of ideas for creating dances; it also extends the boundaries of the concept of dance as art and offers a frame of reference within which the student can organise perceptions of dance works. This is part of Best's 'background', cited on page 9.

Similarly, in the context of performing dances, by making reference to theatre dance examples pupils can become acquainted with the public notion of what constitutes skilfully-executed dance movements through experience of dances performed by professionals. Here, in mainstream theatre dance at least, attributes of good dance posture and body alignments, grace, ease of movement, extra stretch, resilience, pliancy and the full use of body parts or the whole body in numerous dance co-ordinations, dynamically and spatially differentiated, offer exemplary performance targets towards which pupils can strive. This also is part of Best's 'background'.

Equal emphasis on creativity, imagination, individuality and on acquisition of knowledge of theatre dance

With the above reorientations clearly defined, the *midway* model demands knowledge of theatre dance as a prerequisite for creativity, imagination and individuality of expression. To quote Best (1985) again:

> A necessary condition for being creative is to have mastered at least to some extent the discipline, techniques and criteria of a subject or activity.

Feelings and subjectivity versus training and objectivity

Emphasis on feelings

In Ruth Foster's book *Knowing in my Bones* (1976) we find a plea for retaining an emphasis on the uniquely personal experience of the creative act. This must have been the result of the over-emphasis on the *professional* model which she saw in secondary schools and colleges at the time of writing. She states, for example, that:

> The arts are concerned primarily ... with the springs of feeling and its manifestation in various media.

and that:

> In dance, movement takes on very closely the shape of sensation and in turn shapes it. The experience of the dancer is an intimately personal one in which action may be said to be the very fabric of feeling itself.

How exactly movement 'takes on very closely the shape of sensation', or is even associated with sensations in the mind of the composer is not clear. A weakness of the argument rests on the assumption that, along with the memory of feelings, there is a stored-up vocabulary of associated movements. In other words, if the composer recalls the feeling, a ready recipe of movements comes to mind and these are 'the very fabric of feeling itself'. Conversely, certain movements could be found to induce a recall of feelings. This reminds one of Laban's (1948) idea 'that varying emotions can be induced through [the performer's] actions'.

The stress upon the psychological impact of dance on the individual puts Foster (1976) in a clearly supportive position for the *educational* model. It is also evident that she is strongly influenced by Robert Witkin's ideas concerning *The Intelligence of Feeling* (1974). Witkin sees the arts as the creative expression of subjective feeling. He makes a distinction between the public and the private worlds and suggests that, in the school curriculum, the arts are the only means of entering into the latter. The private world is concerned with sensations and feelings and is removed from the object world and factual knowledge. It is also clear, however, that, as noted by Foster (1976), Witkin (1974) does not consider a spontaneous outpouring and simple discharging of feelings to be expressive action. This he describes as reactive behaviour. Rather, it is reflexive action he advocates as that which arts teachers should encourage. By this he means that the pupils should be helped to look inside themselves, respond to their feelings in a reflexive manner and express them in the art medium without reference to the external world or techniques imposed by the teacher. The critics of this view hold that if the artist wants to communicate feelings some account has to be taken of public conventions and shared meanings. As Redfern (1973) says:

> What can be expressed is partly, and perhaps largely determined not only by what others have 'said' but also on how they have 'said it'.

This is not new of course. Langer (1953) wrote that:

> Art is a public possession because the formulation of felt-life is the heart of any culture and moulds the objective world for the people. It is their school of feeling and their defence against outer and inner chaos.

For Witkin in 1974 however, the product is not accountable in the public world. His thesis, reiterated by Foster, lays emphasis once more on the participatory benefits of art on the individual coming to grips with problems and feelings. For example, in discussion on dance composition, Foster almost exclusively concentrates attention on inspirational moments, especially at the start of the creative act, when intuition seems subconsciously to direct the work. She admits that 'a full description of the whole process of composition' is not given. She certainly ignores the cognitive aspects of the creative process.

A more valid view of intuition is provided by Louis Arnaud Reid (1981):

> This intuition is not without conceptualisation. Whatever we apprehend directly is, inescapably apprehended in terms of concepts, infused with, has assimilated an indefinitely large body of knowledge about things, knowledge-that.

Since feelings/intuitions and knowledge are so inextricably linked we can say that we are gaining knowledge through experience of feelings in dance. An interchange of thought and feeling occurs when the pupil experiences the art work in the making. Interaction will not occur unless pupils become aware that movements and form structures can express meaning. Pupils should be led to explore movements and at the same time be encouraged to learn the conventional significance attached to their 'colour', 'texture' and feeling. The initial process in creating a dance is to express a certain feeling; after research or reflection on the feeling to be expressed, the next step is to select from improvisation of new movements and from the learned repertoire of movements associated with that feeling. From the moment that something is made, however, there should be interaction between the pupil's intuition or feeling and knowledge. This is a feeling response to the emerging creative form, a response which is no longer the initial feeling. The feeling that emanates from the process of creating itself – the feeling of 'rightness' – acts as motivation to drive the creative act on. It is not easy to say from where this derives or to dissociate it from knowledge. Maybe, as Reid implies, it is merely old knowledge/experience which has been forgotten but somehow emerges from subconscious depths as an inspirational answer to the creative problem in hand. As Reid (1983) says:

> What is needed is absorption of discursively reflective thinking and study, an assimilation of it, a conscious forgetting of it, and a return to illuminated intuition.

The two kinds of feelings discussed above – those being expressed as the theme of the dance and those which direct the creative process – provide the subjective and individual elements in the composition. However, taking account of Reid's views, we have to conclude that these subjective feelings are cognitive and that feeling and knowing occur simultaneously. To concentrate on the one without the other makes no sense. We should also acknowledge that expression in art emerges as a mix of subjective experience with culturally-derived objective knowledge. Pupils need to learn how to objectify their subjective experiences through the artistic medium.

Emphasis on training

It has already been established that the *professional* model for dance in schools is largely that which in America is termed Modern Dance and in Britain is called Contemporary Dance. Its form, style and conventions, demanding as much discipline and training as Classical Ballet, have become established through several generations of practising artists and teachers. One of the most influential of these, Martha Graham, has been quoted many times in saying that 'it takes ten years to build a dancer. The body must be tempered by hard, definite technique' (1935).

It was this aspect of American Contemporary Dance which came to be promoted in secondary schools and colleges in the late

1960s and early 1970s. Teachers who adopted this model, held that the body, as an instrument, needs to be refined and fashioned for the purpose of art. There was the notion that if pupils created for themselves, using the natural movement of the body (as in Laban's Modern Educational Dance lessons), the movement would not be good enough, not technically refined or advanced enough to be acceptable on an 'art' level.

The teachers therefore adopted a technique, such as Graham's, which through strict discipline imposed a vocabulary of refined movement skills on pupils. Although status and recognition were thus gained in the professional world, teachers soon found that in order to develop such skills successfully it is necessary for pupils to have and maintain what Glasstone (1986) calls 'facility':

> ... a well proportioned body, with easy joint mobility; strong well-shaped, flexible feet; a spine that is both straight and flexible ... attributes ... essential for a dancer to be able to function satisfactorily at a purely mechanical level, enabling him or her to perform the required movements accurately and without physical injury.

Not only is it necessary to have all the physical attributes pre-scribed, pupils need also to be able to adjust to the discipline and demands of training to achieve the heights of correct technical and artistic mastery. It is exceptionally difficult to adhere to the traditional practices, slowly building bodily expertise, and retain individual flair even though prescriptions for success insist that this should be the aim. Because it takes so long to shape and train the body and it is hard work to achieve a standard sufficiently good for artistic performance for an audience in an ordinary once-a-week (or less) school situation, there would be many participants who would never experience this as an end product of their labours. They unfortunately would go no further than perceiving dance as the class exercises or basic training schedules for dancers which they fail to master.

On the other hand, in the spirit of today's approaches to education where there is much greater emphasis on objectives and achievable ends, there is, as the Calouste Gulbenkian Foundation report, *Dance Education and Training in Britain* (1980), states:

> widespread agreement that for older children a higher level of skill acquisition is desirable and that a more structured approach will not kill spontaneity but will increase the power of expression by widening the vocabulary of movement.

However, later the report continues:

> By technique we do not mean here the mastery of skill
> and accuracy in a particular vocabulary of steps and exercises
> in a particular style. Such a concept of technique is too narrow.
> ... Rather we mean by technique the discipline of the art,
> something a child might acquire in three concurrent stages
> – personal development through movement; the acquisi-
> tion of skill in movement; the bringing together of skill and
> personal qualities for an artistic purpose expressed through
> dance.

Clearly, the views expressed here reiterate what has been said above
in respect of the narrow overspecialisation of training the body in
one technique. The shift from an obvious acknowledgement of the
educational model for the primary stage, to an unidentifiable means
of the child becoming skilful in movement and a nebulous bringing
together of these experiences does not help the teacher to understand how to develop performance skills as part of the art of dance
in education. Further on in the report, there is mention of how
specialist help in ballet, etc., may be made available for the talented
few and how dance artists might function in demystifying the art
form. There is some reference to training teachers so that they have
knowledge of techniques, but no conception is offered in the report
as to what kind of technical training is appropriate for schools.

Since the report was published, however, dance examinations,
first CSE, then GCE O and A level, and now, in addition to the
latter, GCSE and AS level, have found ways of objectively testing
technical skills by means of pupils performing set technical studies
in an assessment context. This innovation is largely one to which I
can lay claim and much more detailed discussion of the underlying
theory behind it will be presented in the ensuing chapters.

Skilful dance performance is not the only aspect of the art of dance
in education model which can be assessed objectively. In the GCSE
examination, for example, students present dances to be assessed in
choreographic skills and their dance appreciation is examined
through coursework packages and examination scripts. Hence
all three strands of the art of dance model, creating, performing
and appreciating, offer potential for objective testing. Examples
of assessment will be discussed later in the book, but it is certainly
not easy to define criteria which will be appropriate and sufficiently
flexible to be applicable to all artistic and aesthetic achievements.
Herein lies the problem of overdoing objectivity in the arts.

It could be said then that the *professional* theatre dance model has shown the way towards greater accountability as an antidote to the over-indulgent subjectivity upheld by those perpetuating the *educational* model. But, as shown above, there is need of a much broader definition of the *professional* model than that taken up by dance educators initially with the central interest in technique per se. The broader view of the *professional* model derives from the shift in the conceptual basis towards the art of dance model. Here the whole of the professional artistic world of dance is in focus. The dancers, the dance works – how they are created, rehearsed, interpreted and notated – the choreographers, design, music, lighting, theatrical setting, cultural, historical and social contexts constitute the range of dance study. Knowledge, understanding and skills can be developed and assessment criteria need to be formulated to determine what the pupils know, understand, and can do in the dance art context.

Equal emphasis on feelings and on training

The clearer account of feeling/intuition offered above (as opposed to the view that sensations and feelings are the private domain of the individual into which it is not possible or desirable to intrude), together with broader objectives in stating what can be learned in all three strands – performing, creating and appreciating – provide a degree of balance to the art of dance in education model. This is the most difficult aspect of the conceptual basis to discuss but it is important that teachers and lecturers are constantly aware of the tenuous interplay between feeling and knowing and the dangers of overplaying one at the expense of the other. Keeping such a balance is a persistent theme throughout this book.

Movement principles versus stylised techniques

Emphasis on movement principles

A particular characteristic of the *educational* model is that the dance experience is based upon a set of principles or concepts rather than systematised or graded groups of exercises and skills which constitute a *professional* model. Laban formulated his principles through observation of movement in varying situations. They are general principles of movement, therefore, and not specific to dance. In other words, Laban's system is not codified into set patterns of movement which need to be fed to pupils according to age, ability and expertise. Rather, though there are progressive stages inherent in the application of the principles which Laban organised into sixteen movement themes, the teacher interprets them in his or her own way. It is 'without a preconceived or dictated style' and 'the whole range of the elements of movement is experienced and practised'. (Laban 1948.)

Although his principles of movement are often referred to as an analysis, because movement is broken down into various components, he does this only in a descriptive way. It serves the teacher who wishes to use a free exploratory approach well. Movement is classified into broad concepts, each of which suggests a range which may be explored in different ways by individual pupils.

Fundamentally, Laban put forward the view that movement can be described under four headings: action, effort (now more often called dynamics or qualities of movement), space and relationships. The following questions may give a clue to the meaning of these terms. What action is being done, and with what body parts is it being performed? How do the actions use time and force (quick–strong–slow–delicate) and are they continuous or intermittent? Where in space do the actions begin, move and end? In which ways are the actions related to objects and/or other people? The basic premise is simply that characteristics of body actions alter in varying situations. In dance, every action that the body can perform, according to its expressive purpose, may be variously coloured by how it uses time, energy, flow, space and relationship factors. For example, travelling steps may be light, quick, freely-going, upward and forward to express joy or conversely, heavy, with-held, slow and downward to express sadness.

The benefits of using the principles of movement as a source of content are that the whole range is available, and the choice of movement in dance compositions is likely to be dependent upon the meaning to be conveyed rather than upon a range of already-learned dance movements. The latter are ready-made 'wholes' with specified use of the components of action, dynamics and space, and have defined stylistic properties. Laban's principles, on the other hand, are more valuable for varied expressive purposes because they expose components only and it is up to the dance choreographer to make up the 'wholes' and ascribe a style according to the dance idea. In this respect, the principles can be likened to a paint palette.

Criticisms of the principles as content not surprisingly highlight the lack of technical skill required of pupils. Because they are free to explore their own natural movement range in response to movement tasks, they have no concepts of how to refine movements beyond the everyday into dance. Hence there is probably no extra extension, no projection of focus, no polish in co-ordinations of movements and certainly no particular style. Indeed the movement outcomes were often criticised as self-indulgent wallowing in improvised undifferentiated movement which could be performed by anyone. The artistic and aesthetic concerns for what it looked like were sacrificed for what it felt like for the performer. But really this is not so much a criticism of the principles but how they were employed and the romantic theories attached to them. It is contended here, in the same way as in my book *Dance Composition* (1992), that the principles themselves remain a very useful tool for the art of dance in education model and it will become evident that they can be beneficially employed in teaching all three of the activities – creating, performing and appreciating dances.

Emphasis on stylised techniques

In the above text the word technique is used when discussing the acquisition of physical skill. However, in dance, the term is also used in discussing style. Detailed discussion of the relationship between techniques and styles can be found in my book *Dance Composition* (1992).

In the context of the *professional* model, study of a defined technique as content of dance education would entail participation in technique classes in order to learn a particular range of movement and perfect performance of it with attention given to its particular style. Most often technique classes in the professional dance world are in named techniques – in the contemporary dance context, for example – Graham, Cunningham, Limon, Hawkins techniques to name but a few. Students taking a Graham class will learn the technique and acquire the style through participation in floorwork exercises, standing centre exercises for legs and feet, *barre* work, centre practice including stepping, falling, tilting and balancing, and exercises travelling across the floor including jumps. In most techniques there is a division between performing exercises and dancing sequences or parts of repertoire. Through the former the dancer is gaining physical attributes such as strength, flexibility, balance, posture, alignment, co-ordination and stamina, and in the latter is learning how to present and give expression to the movement by attending to qualities of (for example) rhythm, phrasing, dynamics, spatial patterning and style. Of course, the best technique teachers concentrate on such qualities at all times even whilst the pupils are performing the most mundane of exercises. In fact some techniques require this *performance* approach. The Graham technique, for example, gains such an acclaim from De Mille (1960):

> One reason the Graham technique has such wide-spread appeal is that the exercises . . . induce dancing while strengthening and limbering. Each exercise is a fragment of movement exquisitely devised . . . [students] learn phrasing, dynamics and form whilst working on tendons and breath. The workout is in reality a collection of tiny dances, all lovely, all shaped providing transition to the next group . . . so even . . . start[ing] the first contractions, the student is . . . absorbing performance, technique and what is more subtle, dance form.

It must be clear to all who have experienced such classes, however, that it is necessary to have considerable facility for dance movement (as pointed out by Glasstone (1986) above), and considerable time given to practising the technique before even the most basic of standards is reached. This kind of dance training may be appropriate for intensive dance courses in further or higher education but it certainly is not appropriate for secondary school pupils.

Even at college level, however, study of only one dance technique limits students to the kinds of expression that this particular technique can articulate: the Graham Technique, for example, has a most distinctive style. The same can be said for all techniques because each contains its own strong stylistic character and implicit expressive capacities. Hence, a comprehensive art of dance curriculum should expose students to a range of techniques and styles so that they can select the right combinations for their compositions or consider their own performance with a knowledge of the technical and stylistic characteristics pertinent to the piece they are practising.

In the 1990s, it has become common to study a more generalised technique rather than a prescribed or named technique such as the Graham technique. A contemporary dance class, for example, includes movements emphasising the torso, feet in parallel and movements of isolated parts of the body as well as the whole body. It puts emphasis on the pelvic region and centre initiating and arresting momentum, on floorwork and on extensive variations of dynamics. Phrases of travelling, leaping, tipping and falling emphasise movements into, across and off the floor. Such stylistic flavourings give a mainstream contemporary feel to the class. A different range of movement characteristics and vocabulary would emerge from jazz, classical ballet or Indian classes. Whatever the technique, whether specifically named or a mere general combination of many, the students would be learning a vocabulary of set movements and the style of the technique. Perhaps, as indicated above, the best art of dance education should include experience of many of these techniques/styles so that, as in the case of a music student, the art form is studied as a multifarious and richly-varied phenomenon.

Equal emphasis on movement principles and on stylised techniques

Clearly then, rather than the teacher/lecturer in the art of dance in education context settling on one technique, students need to be equipped with a repertoire of techniques which offers a range of stylistic and expressive possibilities. How such a programme can be considered in the limited time available for dance will be discussed in more detail later but some hints may be appropriate here in that important aspects of the conceptual bases include theatre-based exemplars and pre-choreographed dance studies to teach students about techniques and styles. In developing an ability to perform jazz-like pieces, for example, through learning a jazz-based dance study, students could be exposed to the essential features of a jazz vocabulary – movements initiated and isolated to specific parts of the body such as the hips and shoulders, syncopated rhythms, downward stressed grounded movements with sharp changes of direction and focus – and then, through the study of professional jazz dancers on video perhaps, dramatically advance their learning. The sensation of moving in a jazz-like way seems to be transmitted through seeing it well done into doing it well oneself. Indeed, because it is possible to employ all the jazz-like characteristics in a non-jazz style such as disco, it is essential that the nuances of the style are illustrated through a physical demonstration so that pupils recognise the distinctive textures of jazz dance as opposed to anything else. The importance of visual resources together with experience of ready-made dance studies/snippets of repertoire for students of secondary age and above cannot be over-stressed. However, even young children can extend their range and colour their dance movements with stylistic properties through the use of visual resources such as videos or dance artists in school.

Basic characteristics of Indian dance styles, for example, have been successfully transmitted to six and seven year olds in this manner with much supplementary material in the form of pictures, music, costume and stories. Such a dance education substantiates the rich cultural world in which children live and they come to know more about that world through the experience of dance.

It will also become clear to the reader that the art of dance in education model advocated here puts equal emphasis on developing knowledge and understanding of dance techniques and styles along with principles of movement. The guidelines offered by Laban in the form of a descriptive analysis form the language and concepts shared by all who are participating in the dance experiences. Thus, instead of learning special names of movements such as *arabesque*, *jeté*, spiral and suchlike, students and teachers/lecturers describe the actions with common terms such as balance, jump and twist, and then distinguish the dynamic and spatial characteristics of each of these actions with words such as continuous, quick, sharp, upward and forward. Indeed, the use of this everyday language permits a greater degree of clarity and depth in observing and describing the details of the movements. Just to say *arabesque*, for example, describes only the type of movement, for there are hundreds of ways in which an *arabesque* can be performed. Laban's principles provide the means of detailed description.

Another important use of the principles, especially for the teacher, is in providing frameworks within which pupils explore. Dance composition can be guided by the teacher in that the overall structure and range of content for the dance can be set before the class takes place. A *Happy Dance*, for example, could include a section within which the young pupils make a phrase of bouncy jumps from two feet to two feet. This concept could be thoroughly explored and then, with the idea of happiness uppermost in their imaginations, pupils would be led to select and link their jumping movements to create a suitable phrase within a certain length of music. With older students, too, the principles are very useful in dance-making contexts. If a motif has been created it may well be developed and repeated: the level in space can be changed, dynamics or spatial focus altered or the action content increased. The flexibility of this set of principles as a creative tool for the dance composer (discussed in detail in *Dance Composition* 1992), together with a knowledge of stylistic conventions, provide the balance which will eventually lead towards pupils/students gaining greater autonomy, not only in making dances but in performing and appreciating them, too.

Problem solving versus directed teaching methodologies

Emphasis on problem solving

In the *educational* model, stress on the private and psychological effects of dance upon the dancer has implications for methodology. Such ends can only be achieved through an open, discovery approach in which the individual directs his or her own learning. Discovery learning is effected by the teacher who presents a problem-solving situation which delineates an area for exploration by the pupil. For example, a task such as 'move quickly, turn, rise and fall', can lead the student into many varieties of quick movement, many ways of turning and so on, some of which may be original discoveries for the individual. Members of the class, therefore, would not all be performing the same movement, but would be working inventively within the confines of the task or dance idea and of their abilities, both physical and imaginative. The teacher's role in this situation is a difficult one:

> The dance teacher not only sets up the situation and suggests the material to be explored, but through suggestion and questions opens up a world of possibilities to be experienced by the child. . . . The teacher therefore acts as guide rather than director.
> (Russell 1974)

Whilst pupils work individually or in groups in order to find their movement answers to movement tasks, the teacher draws attention to variety and/or quality of content from what is observed and aims to improve responses in these terms by means of suggestions, practises and demonstrations. As Foster (1977) states, 'it is not easy to become a catalyst in the creative process' but, essentially, this was the role of the teacher in the *educational* model. However, as Foster goes on to say, this methodology poses problems for evaluation. First, in respect of the problems set: how does the teacher assess what is good and what is trivial? Also, how may progression be ensured for each pupil?

What seemed to be missing in the *educational* model were standards, levels and publicly acceptable frames of reference. Even in the context of creating dance movement there was a difficulty in that, in the main, publicly acknowledged aesthetic criteria for art criticism was not a part of the teacher's knowhow. Guidance of the creative act, therefore, remained an insular private event between a teacher/lecturer and a group. Decisions as to what was good were made without reference to relevant theatre models or examples on video or film. So it would appear that it was not so much the dominance of open-ended teaching styles that caused problems but the overall lack of knowing what ends these methods were achieving. As Foster (1977) says, unless clear ends are identified, there is danger that this method:

> leads to children not approaching creative heights, but settling for an inadequate destination. Neither is the goal of merely approaching. It should contain an element of achieving as well.

Nevertheless, there is a clear relationship between the philosophical bases of the *educational* model and approaches to teaching which lead pupils to become agents in their own learning. Although texts supporting this model advocate a range of teaching strategies, their authors definitely urge teachers away from didactic methods or intrusion and aim to persuade the teacher to take on the role of stimulator and catalyst rather than knowledgeable expert.

Emphasis on directed teaching

De Mille (1960) said that 'the best way of learning is still apprenticeship under a professional' and, in the 1990s, in professional training contexts in all the performing arts, this seems still to be the case. In teaching the named techniques, for example, the teacher needs to be an expert in the sense of knowing and thoroughly understanding the range of exercises and patterns of movement which have evolved as the content of the dance style. It is also necessary to know how best to instruct so that learning is effected in the most economical way. The teacher as an instructor enforces what is to be done, how it is to be done, for how long the practice will take place and the standard it reaches. The learner must be disciplined, succumb to teacher control and work towards optimum physical performance. This is teacher-centred education.

Equal emphasis on problem solving and on directed teaching

It will become evident in the following chapters that the successful teacher must be able to employ both these kinds of teaching strategies and many combinations of them.

The open-ended problem-solving approach is most readily associated with creative dance-composing situations as illustrated above, but it is also important for pupils to learn how to improve their own and others' dance performances through, for example, writing a checklist of things to look for in good performance and using this to comment critically upon their individual performances on video or those of peers in the live situation. The teacher here acts as catalyst, guide and consultant, rather than instructor. For the appreciation of professional dance works it is also very important that teachers/lecturers frequently employ an open-ended non-instructive method of teaching. Here, students' perceptions need to be guided rather than directed because they must interpret the meanings/feelings in the works in their own way. There are many different ways in which such guidance can be effected through setting the students to research in books, to study critics' opinions and to write their own to respond to questions about the work seen, to discuss or to write about certain aspects of it, and so on. In all of these activities students are required to think for themselves and are not *given* information. The aim is that they come to know the works for themselves and can back up their own views about them with clearly-argued reasons. More on this later.

The closed instructive approach should also be used at appropriate times in the art of dance in education model. This is especially the case where acquisition of skills or initiation into new ways of thinking is concerned. Pring, as far back as 1976 for example, states that:

> learning . . . should be seen much more as a kind of apprenticeship than it normally is – learning how to do something alongside the successful practitioner, by imitating, by subjecting oneself to correction and to direction.

This didactic approach is becoming fashionable again whilst progressive methods are under scrutiny. Certainly in the art of dance in education model it has its place but the implication is that the teacher should be a good dancer with training and experience in performing and also with an ability to demonstrate clearly, to explain carefully, and to observe quickly and correctly.

Moreover, the teacher should also have been a choreographer of some note if the role of expert in this context is to be assumed. Perhaps this is where dance artists can play an important role in imparting high-level technical training and teaching repertoire in 'master class' experiences for students. Certainly, artists most often use a directed teaching method and, if properly prepared, the students' learning can progress dramatically under such expert guidance.

FEATURES OF THE MIDWAY MODEL

The following table demonstrates how, in my view, elements of the *educational* and *professional* models have been absorbed, albeit in much altered form, into a new model for teaching dance in education. The *midway* model, however, as stated previously, has distinctive features of its own.

Table to demonstrate features of the art of dance in education model

EDUCATIONAL	MIDWAY	PROFESSIONAL
Process	Process + Product	Product
Creativity Imagination Individuality	Creativity Knowledge of Imagination + public artistic Individuality conventions	Knowledge of theatre dance repertoire
Feelings Subjectivity	Feelings + Skill Subjectivity + Techniques	Skill acquired Objectivity
Principles	Principles + Techniques	Techniques
Open methods	Open + Closed	Closed methods
Creating	THREE STRANDS Composition Performance Appreciation OF DANCES leading to ARTISTIC EDUCATION AESTHETIC EDUCATION CULTURAL EDUCATION	Performing

The three strands: creating, performing, appreciating

These three processes constitute the conceptual basis of the *art of dance in education* model. Most of the current literature reinforces this. It is my view, however, that the term 'appreciating' should not be used to describe the third process involved in dance education. Its meaning is more all-embracing than this. Appreciation in an art context can be defined as an ability to perceive and value the qualities in an object. Full appreciation of the features in the art work – its expression, form and style, together with admiration of the cleverness, precision and originality with which it has been wrought – can produce a sense of enjoyment, sometimes even elation.

> The enjoyment and emotion, however, are not identical with what the use of the terms in ordinary discourse and everyday experiences denotes although they could not exist or develop without roots in that experience.
>
> (Broudy 1972)

The key to this enjoyable appreciation resides in the object itself and in the depth of feeling and understanding the perceiver brings to the experience of it. Hence, 'appreciation' is the term to use when the perceiver comes to value an art work for the artistic, aesthetic and/or cultural qualities and meanings it has for him or her. In the art of dance in education context, such an appreciation will emerge as a result of much experience in creating, performing and viewing dances.

The conceptual basis of the art of dance model, for me then, might be illustrated thus:

THROUGH

CREATING

PERFORMING

VIEWING

The **processes** involved in the art of dance in education – creating, performing and viewing dances – describe what the pupils/students do in their dance lessons/lectures.

The **products** – dance compositions, dance performances and dance appreciation – are the outcomes of their learning and it is these products that can be assessed.

The dance programmes of study in the National Curriculum clearly state what it is expected that pupils will achieve in each of the key stages, and GCSE, AS and A level together with BTEC and degree course in dance also assess or examine dance compositions, dance performances and dance appreciation. The last is most often assessed through written work though there are other ways in which appreciation can be evaluated. Perhaps the most obvious way to arrive at the outcome of in-depth appreciation of dance works is through learning how to compose and perform dances oneself. The knowledge, understanding and artistic sensitivity gained from composing and performing dances underpins and augments knowledge and understanding gained from viewing dances. That is why the diagram above shows appreciation as an 'umbrella' concept, an ultimate aim, for dance education which results from qualitative experiences of the processes of performing, creating and viewing dances.

In my view, the conceptual basis for the art of dance in education has been defined and explained in many texts incorrectly in that the three strands have been called creating, performing and appreciating. These are verbs to describe the processes involved in dance education. But appreciating is not a process it is an outcome. Hence, as the diagram above demonstrates, appreciation is constantly being developed through all three processes – creating, performing and viewing.

The logical conclusion of this argument is to be clear as to whether it is the process or the product that is being described. As stated above, whilst it is certainly possible to arrive at a product of a dance composition through the process of creating and a product of a dance performance through the process of performing, the product of appreciation is not gained through viewing alone. Appreciation is an overall outcome.

Nonetheless, even though the above definition of appreciating clearly indicates a more complex meaning, it has become common parlance in dance education to use the word as the third strand. Other art forms use different terms. For example, music in the National Curriculum refers to listening and appraising. In the context of dance education, however, appreciating has become linked with processes of viewing, responding, describing, analysing, interpreting and evaluating dances and learning about dance and its history.

In adherence to this common practice in dance education, therefore, the term appreciating is used throughout this book. Rather than change it for the sake of accuracy, readers are asked to keep in mind the broader definition of appreciation as an outcome of the three processes – creating, performing and viewing dances – whenever the term is used.

Artistic education

The processes of creating, performing and viewing dances and the overall appreciation gained from these experiences can be defined as artistic education in that the learner is coming to know more about the art form itself. So far in this text the concepts of artistic and aesthetic education have been coupled. Indeed, it is difficult to disentangle artistic from aesthetic education since, in all dance art experiences they are interdependent but, for the purposes of clarity, it is suggested here that the artistic aspects of dance education tend to be those which are learned in an objective way, those which relate to the discipline of dance.

A discipline-based education in the art of dance is concerned with developing the students' skills, knowledge and understanding. Physical dance skills are developed in performance. Choreographic skills are developed through creating one's own dances and learning from dances created by others. Appreciation skills are developed through learning how to view dances, how to describe, interpret and evaluate them. Of course these skills cannot develop without knowledge and understanding of the concepts involved in creating and performing dances. Skills, knowledge and understanding cannot be separated and developed in a linear manner. Rather they develop simultaneously in a balanced art of dance education.

In order to distinguish the nature of artistic education however, we need to consider the range of concepts involved in creating, performing and appreciating dances.

The central requirement is that an understanding of the nature of a dance develops throughout the experience of dance education. The concept of a dance will constantly change. For the younger pupils it may simply be thought of as a collection of movements, patterned in time and space to create a form with a beginning, middle and end. This is suggested in the National Curriculum programme of study for dance at key stage 1. For the university student it is impossible to produce any one definition since the concept of what a dance is differs considerably in terms of historical/cultural context and artistic *milieu*. Nonetheless, understanding of dances as artefacts each with distinguishing features is an essential aspect of artistic education. The art object or product, usually intended for an audience, is the main focus.

Most of the concepts and skills developed through the processes of creating, performing and viewing dances can be labelled artistic. The following lists are not intended to be comprehensive but are useful in determining what is meant by the term *artistic education*.

Artistic learning at the level appropriate to the learner's experience/age through:

Creating dances

- understanding of and interpretation of themes/ideas
- translation of themes/ideas into dance terms, i.e into symbolic action
- making decisions about the type of dance, e.g. dramatic, pure, comic, abstract, and about the style, e.g contemporary, balletic, jazzy
- exploration of movement ideas, discovering actions, qualities, rhythmic and spatial features to express the theme in the type and style of dance planned
- exploring and making decisions about the numbers of dancers and the relationship possibilities needed to express the idea, e.g. positioning, group shapes, orchestration
- understanding of how the music or accompaniment can be used
- selecting and linking movements to make motifs and phrases
- stylising content appropriately
- deciding the order of movements and refining motifs and phrases
- structuring motifs and phrases in time and space, and the relationship between dancers
- developing the phrases, perhaps repeating them in time, space and relationship configurations
- understanding the use of formal devices: repetition, development, contrast, transition, progression, unity or alternative construction processes such as chance
- creating sections or parts of the dance and combining them to make a whole dance
- considering staging aspects of dances: lighting, design, costume, make-up, use of accompanying visual/audio materials, etc.

• presenting dances in conventional/alternative spaces with consideration of the role of the audience: programme notes, etc.

Performing dances ·

• acquiring physical skills: actions combined with dynamic, rhythmic and spatial patterning or stylistically defined skills from specific techniques
• performing the above with co-ordination, accuracy, fluency, control, balance, poise and confidence
• practising co-ordination in movements to link phrases, sections and dances
• performing the content concentrating on qualitative expression through variation of dynamic, spatial and relationship features
• performing dances and parts of dances with understanding of the formal qualities, e.g. pauses, highlights, contrasts
• presenting the theme through dancing expressively
• practising dance to music or other forms of accompaniment alone or with others in unison and canon
• developing performance qualities such as extension, projection and focus in order to express meaning
• concentrating on line, body shape, clarity of design, positioning
• showing clarity and unity of style

Viewing dances

• observing, describing, analysing and evaluating all the aspects involved in creating and performing (such viewing by students of their own and professional choreography should take place throughout dance education)

These three processes, creating, performing and viewing dances, will develop the ability to appreciate artistic features of dances.

Appreciation of artistic aspects of dance

• students will learn to discern with increasing accuracy and sensitivity a range of qualities in choreography and performance. Through analogy with their own experiences in choreography and performance and through learning how to employ description, interpretation and evaluation they will be able to perceive distinctive artistic features: style, form, expression, techniques and production

• in order to further appreciation, students will learn to employ a range of resources to discover background information and specific details about dances, choreographers, performers, designers and musicians

Aesthetic education

Aesthetic perception, though probably something with which we are all endowed, needs, like other kinds of perception, to be nurtured and developed. The individual learns to use sense modalities in increasingly differentiated ways and to organise the complex sensory world by use of different frames of reference. However, it is not through a simple process of maturing that we are able to use an aesthetic frame of reference. We need to learn to attend to the contained qualities in dance rather than the mere physicalities of bodies in action. What these qualities in art may be and how they may be related is, in essence, what aesthetic education in dance is about.

Aesthetic education is essentially an education of feeling. In the aesthetic qualities of a work of art we receive an experience of the feelings embodied. For example, we often attribute human feelings/meanings to music we hear (sad music perhaps) and the dances we see (an angry dance, maybe). Through appreciation of their various dynamic, temporal and spatial 'textures' students of dance should become aware of the expressive power of movements and their juxtaposition. Movements kinesthetically felt, can become increasingly differentiated in tone and texture if the students become sensitive to the elements and combinations of elements, which yield insights into human feeling. Furthermore, thinking about symbolic meaning in movement and learning about its components and significance should occur alongside feeling it.

How then do we guide and develop this education of feeling? As indicated above, an aesthetic frame of reference may be useful here for teachers. But is there such a thing? It is certainly difficult to accommodate these two seemingly conflicting notions: first, that each piece of art has its own meanings, and second that general principles or categories of aesthetic judgment exist within a single frame of reference. It is naive to suppose that the essences of all works of art, throughout time, can be distilled and appraised by one single uniform method. Moreover, art works are viewed subjectively by individuals in distinctive ways. Nevertheless, description and evaluation as Reid (1969) says 'need to be held together in some general framework (even if it is a flexible one); if not it will tend to degenerate into loose talk about personal impressions'. What is needed then, is a general framework which allows for individual subjectivity of feeling yet classifies aesthetic qualities in works of art in general terms so that discussion of them may be shared.

Osborne (1970) classifies aesthetic qualities under the headings of sensory qualities, expressive qualities and formal qualities. The sensory qualities which pertain to movement are infinite and a problem of language is immediately encountered when one is asked to detail the qualities perceived in a dance. Not only are there never adequate words, but there is a tendency not to notice that for which we have no language. Where there are no words, training is needed to enable the perceiver to see. This is a skill which needs to be developed if the ability to appreciate is to be attained.

In dance there is always the danger that perceived movements become named (e.g. *arabesque* in ballet and 'contraction' in contemporary dance). It is, therefore, important that teachers extend their pupils' understanding of movements in sensory terms so that, for example, the qualities of an *arabesque* could be described as linear, balanced, flowing, angular, curving, smooth, arrested or lingering according to how it is performed. Just to name a movement is not enough because the same action can be performed with various qualities which in turn create different aesthetic feelings in the onlooker. The teacher then, should help students to notice and attend to sensory qualities, which may be called the superstructure of the overall aesthetic.

Expressive qualities are emergent features of sensory qualities and again language for naming them is crude. A further problem is that there is no special language to describe expressive qualities of works of art as distinct from human emotions and expressions. Hence, human sadness is attributed to a dance which appears sad. Of course it is not possible to attribute particular expressive qualities to particular movements, because their meanings become different in different contexts and juxtapositions. However, there are some general pointers – for example, that curves in space can denote gentleness, that one person high and upright with several others at his feet may denote power and submission. Care should always be taken not to *fix* correlating ideas and movements, since their expressiveness depends upon their role in each individual dance.

The aesthetic qualities which are called formal are denoted by such terms as unity, balance, integration, harmony, texture, proportion, contrast, etc. Here, older students could be guided to follow motifs consciously and to appreciate the intricacies of development, variation, combination, deconstruction and reconstruction that they go through in order to create the unified form. They could also consider how sections of dances are proportioned and balanced in relationship to each other, how the rhythmic 'time picture' is presented in terms of quiet moments, activity, transition, climax, and how spatial patterning is rhythmic, asymmetric, formal, intricate, for example.

If the teacher can develop devices for presenting the aesthetic aspects of dance, students may gradually come to view dance with deep and creative contemplation. Furthermore, concentration on sensory, expressive and formal aesthetic qualities in art works directs attention away from evaluations which bear no reference to the art work itself.

In aesthetic education then, we have a situation in which as Gibson (in Abbs 1989) says:

> feelings show us the limits of our language. They bring home to us that language is not omnicompetent; for we know far more than we can say. It is when we try to put into words our feelings, when we attend to explore our inner states (states that vividly and significantly exist, have reality and are of profound consequences for action) that the gap between language and experience is starkly exposed. It is at such moments we must turn to poets and artists, not scientists, for genuine illumination. Those understandings are rarely or never fully recoverable in written or spoken language, but it is common experience that they are nonetheless both grasped and valid.

Aesthetic education, the education of feeling is an intangible and immeasurable aspect of dance education. As Gibson goes on to say:

> Feelings have puzzling relationships with time. They are processes not products: they have, in their intense here-and-now sense, a fleetingness and fugitiveness in their experience and expression. They are grasped and intuited only in their moments of experiencing ... Such experiences are of the present to be enjoyed at the time. They are not future-oriented and not rewarded with grades or certificates. It is with this present, shared, experienced, nature of emotions in mind that we return to the question of the education of feeling.

The education of feeling may not be measurable, yet it is very important that it is not lost or put aside in favour of what can be assessed. Those teaching the art of dance need to keep in mind a framework such as that of Osborne described on page 32, in order that it underpins dance experiences.

Cultural education

According to Reid (1986), the first approach to an art work cannot be 'intellectual' or 'conceptual':

> We cannot come to know and understand works of art first from the top of the head, and then downwards. Experience, feeling, direct, particular, concrete, comes first; intellectual analysis, perhaps later.

This puts emphasis on aesthetic education before other kinds of education. However, through the art of dance, it is also important to encourage understanding of culture amongst the young. Art is an important aspect of culture, and should therefore be valued not only for its aesthetic and artistic character but as a teacher of and about culture.

Western culture is, of course, the predominant focus of the art of dance model, whose roots are in Western theatre dance. The form, style and expression of a theatre dance work reflect Western traditions and ideologies and can therefore be analysed as a semiotic picture of Western culture. Such a study of theatre dance as a complex sign system is perhaps the province of higher education, yet, from an early age, children should learn that Western theatre dance is distinct from other cultural forms. Whilst it is possible to 'read' universal messages in some dance movements, there are particular meaning connotations attached to dance vocabulary, too. An *arabesque* in ballet and a 'contraction' in contemporary dance have in-built Western meanings. Moreover, contemporary dance choreographers often employ everyday gestures with their culturally-defined meanings to form the basis of expression. Pupils therefore need to be able to apply their understanding of non-verbal communication in Western culture to dance works of this type. In the Western world, for example, we understand that the hitch hiker's thumb jerk calls for a lift but the thumb jerk has very different meanings in other contexts! Increasingly then, pupils should become appreciative of the cultural meanings, artistic traditions, style and presentation of choreography in the theatre and of how such meanings, traditions and styles have developed.

Understanding the history of an art form as part of Western society is therefore an essential aspect of cultural education. Through such study pupils will become aware of the meanings of terms such as *contemporary dance, classical, neo-classical, romantic ballet* and *post-modern dance,* and appreciate the ways in which the art works themselves signify changes and developments in the practice of dance. Knowledge of the history of the art of dance needs to be supported by study of the political, social and philosophical ideas at the times and places from which the dance works emerge. In this way students will appreciate them as ever-changing cultural phenomena.

Although Western culture is rich in artistic achievement and there is much to learn about the traditions and practices that underpin all the various kinds of theatre dance, there are other dance cultures to be learned about. As stated in *Dance in Schools*:

> We live in a multicultural society. Dance is a prime expression of culture, of heritage, identity and achievement. The richer the diversity of cultures within a given community, the richer the dance can be. Pupils can share their various dance heritages through traditional dances and they may bring into school a rich movement vocabulary and different understanding of dance.
>
> Arts Council (1993)

This suggests that a typical group in any sector of education will have pupils of different cultural backgrounds working together and that teachers should make sure that a range of dance forms is experienced.

The art of dance model puts an emphasis on Western dance forms but it can be appropriate (as professional choreographers demonstrate) to integrate dance forms from other cultures in Western dance works. An example of this in contemporary dance is Jiri Kylian's *Stamping Ground* which derived from a close study of aboriginal dance and an integration of some attributes of this form with that of contemporary dance. The practice of mixing different dance forms creates new and interesting outcomes, reflecting the cultural richness of a community in art works. Students at school and college should be able to bring their own dance vocabularies, including social dance vocabularies, into the processes of creating dances. The greater the range of movement content and the more cultural influences entering the dance experience, the better it reflects our multicultural society.

A comprehensive experience in the art of dance will not only include the use of different ethnic and social dance forms; it will give some attention to different groups in society who participate in the art of dance. For example, it is becoming more accepted that disabled people can perform as dance artists in the same ways as able-bodied dancers. *Candoco* is a prime example of success in this context. Also, community dance workers demonstrate that the árt of dance does not have to take place in the theatre with trained dancers. There are more and more groups performing in non-conventional places and including audience/non-dance participants in the outcome.

Cultural education in the art of dance thus takes account of all of the above concerns.

RESOURCE-BASED TEACHING

The *midway* art of dance model demands a resource-based teaching methodology as the central and most important approach. Clearly, as indicated in the preceding text, this is because of the focus on public dance art works as references for teaching and learning in dance education. The aspects of the *professional* dance model which have been retained and reoriented in the art of dance model (see Table 1 on page 6) give professional dance works a new importance as essential resources for dance in education. In discussion of each of these aspects, there has been illustration of ways in which professional dance exemplars may be employed to develop the pupils' performing, creating and appreciation skills in the art of dance.

An analysis of the theory underpinning resource-based teaching of dance composition can be found in *Dance Composition* (1992). To avoid repetition, the following text provides a rationale for the approach and explains briefly how a professional dance resource may be employed in primary, secondary and higher education.

A good professional example demonstrates artistic and aesthetic quality in its composition and its performance. It also has implicit cultural and historical significance. Although a dance cannot be frozen in time for the purposes of study, video facilities and, in future, compact discs, permit repeated viewings of sections or of the whole work in order to study it as an example of creative, original and qualitative choreography/performance and/or a token of a particular time and place.

It has been witnessed many times in my own practice across the sectors – from primary to higher education – that in-depth study of a work, even a small part of it, enhances, consolidates, extends and inspires the students' own work. A dance work, employed for these reasons is much more than a stimulus. Like a classic novel in the study of English literature, it becomes a starting point for the pupil's own creativity, a means of learning more about the discipline *per se*: style, form, expression, stage/costume/lighting design and performance. Studying a choreographer's interpretation of a theme may extend the student's understanding and awareness of such issues. A dance work can also be studied as an example of choreographic traditions or trends and of the cultural context from which the art work and the choreographer emerge.

Consequently, all the entries under the heading of artistic learning on pages 30–1 can be augmented through the appropriate use of dance works in resource-based teaching/learning activities.

Moreover, if the engagement with an art work is feelingful in the sense that the individual's own feelings and emotions can enter the processes, then it can be labelled an aesthetic experience. In my view, aesthetic interaction between pupils and art works is an important aim for resource-based teaching/learning; teachers/lecturers should ensure that their students' perceptions of sensory, expressive and formal qualities in art works are awakened and developed through the tasks they are given.

Resource-based teaching will work well if the resources selected are appropriate to the objectives of the lessons/lectures, rich in artistic, aesthetic and cultural features and used in balance with other activities within a total programme. In most instances, dance works should not be studied in their every detail (perhaps A level study is the exception) nor analysed with infinite precision. This kind of scrutiny kills the artistic and aesthetic dimensions of the work and makes the study into a pseudo-scientific chore. It serves no purpose unless the intention is to reconstruct the work. If this is the case, the detailed analysis is a means to an end: a reconstructed section or whole dance *re-interpreted* in the students' own way. Hence, as in music, analysis of a professional performance of a work serves only as a qualitative example. It cannot and should not be copied exactly, rather it acts as a detailed reference text against which the students place their own interpretations. In other words, a dance ready-made is a resource to be employed in support of the students' own learning. It is not a set formula to be learned by rote and copied exactly. Neither is it a supply of content for the students' own choreography. This amounts to choreographic plagiarism! Rather, in my experience, the movement vocabulary and choreo-

graphic techniques in a dance work resource should become part
of a bank or repertoire of ideas for the students from which they
select and develop in their own ways. Making the movements or
choreographic principles your own is a very important principle
to maintain in resource-based learning.

The above makes clear the rationale for a resource-based teaching/
learning approach in the art of dance in education model. It should
not be the only approach though. Students and, more particularly,
children need to derive their ideas and inspirations for choreography
from their own imaginations, from other stimuli such as poetry,
etc., and from dance experience itself. They should also learn much
from the teacher/lecturer and from their peers. Moreover, dance
works *per se* are not the only resources applicable to dance education.
Films such as *Singing in the Rain* (an example used in the section on
primary education) *West Side Story* and *Fantasia* are appropriate
resources, too. In these examples, the dance movement and choreography itself are used as a means of teaching/learning something
more about dance. Films on natural phenomena, such as volcanoes,
the sea, animals and insects are better described as very good stimuli
for dance and are therefore not of the same order as the former
resources for resource-based teaching/learning programmes.

However, in order to learn from complex and highly developed
examples of dance works, pupils need to be guided through structured tasks which are sufficiently open for them to make their own
responses to the art work, yet structured enough to aid progression
and constructive learning. The following methods may help achieve
these objectives.

Viewing tasks

Watching dance is difficult. Movements are transient, illusive and
complex. The view of dancers on video is two-dimensional, though,
of course, the movement itself is three-dimensional. The spatial
canvas of dance is never visible – it has to be imagined by the viewer.
A simple example of this non-visible and abstract nature of spatial
patterning is a dancer travelling on a circular pathway – the circle is
not there, it is constructed by the viewer while the dancer travels.
For these and other reasons, the teacher/lecturer needs to help
learners to *see* the dance as it passes through time.

In order to do this without the students being told what to see,
however, it is necessary to provide frameworks or leading questions
to guide perception. It would be quite wrong in an artistic/aesthetic

context to determine exactly what they should notice by directive means. Hence, a student-centred approach is beneficial for most of the viewing tasks.

Methods can include use of teacher-prepared questions (which may be presented in discussion or on work cards), requiring students to observe, make comparisons, describe, interpret and make evaluative comment on what they see. For example, in relation to the initial 'ghosts' dance in Christopher Bruce's *Ghost Dances*, they might be asked to observe and describe the movement of the ghosts' heads in relation to their bodies and to suggest why Bruce selected such actions. This requires observation, description and interpretation. The next task might require the students to note how these head movements are repeated and developed throughout the section and then they might be asked to make evaluative comments on the ways in which the choreographed head movements enhanced the meaning/feeling and at the same time produced form in the ghost section of the dance work. Such questions lead rather than direct the students in their viewing but they also leave a broad scope for possible interpretations.

Alternatively, a multiple choice type of question on a work card could offer a range of possible words to describe the qualities in a phrase of movements, asking the students to select the most appropriate and perhaps to add their own to the given list. This helps the students to develop language to describe what is seen and also subtly opens their eyes to the range of qualities in the movements studied. Younger pupils might be asked for words to describe these qualities and the teacher could write them on the board. Children and students alike should be encouraged to use analogies and metaphors to make clear their perceptions of sensory and expressive qualities.

On almost every occasion of viewing a work, students should have opportunity to reflect on or talk about the feelings that the work evokes in them. These feelings could be positive or negative, but should be backed by reasoned comments. Articulating feelings, even if only for the students' own benefit, is important if the art of dance is to contribute effectively to aesthetic education.

Viewing tasks are often necessary precursors of performing and creating tasks since the dance work resource is the starting point for such work in resource-based teaching/learning.

Performing tasks

A most beneficial way of 'getting inside' a dance work, especially for older students, is to dance the whole or parts of the work. In order to learn a section, for example, the teacher or, occasionally, a dance artist might employ a directed teaching approach so that the students replicate as accurately as possible the choreographed movements. Use of notation, graphics and slow motion video to demonstrate the qualitative aspects of the professional dancers' performance enhances the learning process. However, once the piece is learned this instructive approach should end because students need to colour the movements in their own ways to express the perceived choreographic intention.

This kind of experience is a very valuable way of coming to know a work. To be able to dance a piece of professional choreography, it is necessary to learn how to perform the actions and the rhythmic, dynamic, spatial and relationship patterning in order to understand how the choreographer expresses the idea. Without altering the style and content of the work, the students then have to make their performances their own so that they show understanding of the 'text' through their presentation. The resource, then, constitutes a professional and expert example with which the students can compare and check their own work.

Methods of using the video as a resource have already been mentioned above. There is need for resource packs based on the works of established choreographers. Using compact disc technology, such packs would allow the user access to a bank of computer-programmed data (front and back view video, notation, stills, graphics of floor pattern and body shape for example, close-ups from different angles). Until such packs become available, teachers and lecturers need to design their own ways of teaching dance performance with the aid of videos. A good VHS recorder which holds the picture still enough to discuss the positioning of the limbs (the head and shoulders, for example) and which can be moved frame by frame, helps the analysis of the movement and of course notation confirms the detail. Unfortunately, however, there is little access to notated scores and most teachers/lecturers have insufficient skill in reading notation. In my view, literacy in dance notation will grow when there are enough resource packs containing scores!

To date then, teachers/lecturers should develop their own ways of teaching performance in a resource-based context. Many viewing tasks need to be integrated with performing tasks. For instance, a group might be asked to observe and make a graphic representation of the time-force-accent content of a phrase before attempting to dance it. The students would then learn the sequence having first gained understanding of its qualitative content. Learning becomes much faster and better consolidated if performance grows hand in hand with understanding of the 'text'.

Teachers/lecturers might also create a dance study based upon aspects in the dance work, thus providing a means of working on some of its 'essences' at the students' own level. This 'technical study' approach will be discussed in greater detail in the chapters on the art of dance in secondary and higher education, but perhaps it is important to say here that an adaptation or 'watered down' version of the real thing might be a better way of getting something like the feeling of the work through performance into the students' experience, than attempting to perform movements which are technically beyond their capabilities. As with music, simplified adaptations of parts of dance works taught to students might prove to be a helpful way of 'getting inside' them through learning and performing them.

Creating tasks

There are many ways in which a dance ready-made can be employed as a basis for creative work. Young children may be asked to recall one or two movements and talk about them and then to create their own versions of them. Older pupils may learn a part of a phrase and then end it in their own way, building on and perhaps developing the material. Secondary students, for example, may view a section noting the kinds of leaning and counter balance actions the pairs of dancers are using and extract them to use in their own choreography. University students may study the style of movement or choreographic devices used and extract the essence of the style and/or the principles behind the choreographic devices for use in their own work.

Numerous examples could be given here, but the above are perhaps sufficient to indicate to the reader the advantages of resource-based teaching in developing the students' creative abilities in choreography. Learning from 'givens', i.e. choreographically rich examples (as discussed in the text above on creativity and imagination), and working on these bases towards something new, individual and of creative value depend upon a student's coming to know and understand the discipline/techniques of the art form through in-depth study of its art works. Moreover, carefully formulated tasks which guide the students' perceptions of the way in which the dance work has been choreographed will teach them as much if not more about the processes than practical choreography experiences themselves. Thus artistic and aesthetic appreciation of the choreographer's skill and originality should be a primary objective in all resource-based teaching/learning creating tasks.

Historical/cultural context tasks

This kind of study is important for older students in that in order to understand a dance work they need to put it into a context of time and place. As indicated above, a study of dance works as historical phenomena provides students with knowledge of the practices, trends, styles and genres evident at any one time and of changes that here occurred over time. A study of dance works as cultural products provides students with an understanding of characteristic features of the works and their place in history. Looking inwards at the art work itself and looking outwards at the society from which it emerged, provide a problem-solving means of study whereby students interpret evidence in dance works in the light of their research about the choreographers and the cultures in which the works were created.

Multiple resources are needed in this context. Through reading about works, watching them and making critical comparisons and contrasts, the students gradually become aware of classifications of genre and style and also recognise that some works do not fit easily into such classifications. The students should be led to support their study of a dance resource with research into books, programmes, choreographers' writings or interviews, critics' writings and television documentaries, photographs and any published views of the dancers. Any opportunities to work with the choreographers or dancers themselves would be very beneficial. Such a mixture of primary and secondary sources should offer multiple means of looking *into* the dance works. At the same time, however, such study should be complemented with study of external influences – political, social, economic and cultural – which affect and are reflected in the choreographers' works. Characteristics of the works can then be better understood and explained.

Resource packs

The above approach indicates a need for resource packs containing a variety of materials in addition to a video performance of the dance work studied. Moreover, if resource-based teaching/learning is to be fully effective, activities should be student-centred so that individually or in groups students build up their knowledge of a dance by working through the pack systematically. For example, work cards could direct them to read biographical excerpts from books, newspaper articles, etc., and then to answer questions which require them to reflect on the content or style of the dance work; for instance, in relation to information gained about a choreographer's background.

A comprehensive pack would contain the following:

• a video of the work (including detailed analysis of parts if possible)
• a documentary programme or commentary on the work if available
• a chronology of the choreographer's work and the dates and places of their premières
• video snippets of other works by the choreographer if available
• written materials about the work, about the choreographer, about the dancers, the designer/s, the music and the composer if appropriate
• notated scores of the dance and music
• photographs showing costumes and designs
• press cuttings about the dance, the choreographer, the dancers and the company
• writings about the historical/cultural influences on the work and/or references to books or other sources from which information can be gathered.

In addition, and of great importance, the pack should contain work cards with progressive viewing, performing, creating and historical/cultural study tasks for the students to undertake. Through these means, the students will develop their appreciation of the dance works studied.

Conclusion

The preceding text has presented a theoretical basis for the art of dance in education. The *midway* model which derives from and combines the best features of both the *educational* and *professional* models has been shown to have distinctive features of its own. Its three stands, creating, performing, and viewing dances culminate in appreciation of the art of dance. It also confirms the kinds of education towards which the art of dance strives to contribute i.e. artistic, aesthetic and cultural education. Resource-based teaching/learning, has been presented as an approach which focuses on the study of established dance works at the core of its rationale.

The art of dance in education model has developed over a period of time. However, like all teaching/learning models, it is not static. Teachers should reflect on and develop their own practice so that dance teaching is always dynamic and responsive to change.

The following chapters give some suggestions as to how the theoretical basis described above underpins practice in teaching the art of dance in primary and secondary schools and in higher education. Because the central concern of this book is to provide teachers with a theoretical basis for their work, the headings used in chapter 1 provide the structure for each of the following chapters. The practical examples, however, should further elucidate the theory, a reciprocal relationship between theory and practice being the ideal outcome.

2

The Art of Dance in Primary Schools

Background – a shift towards the art of dance

Young children love to move to music and when they perform movements expressing qualities or moods apparent in the music we often say they are dancing. Indeed we say this when watching birds courting, insects round a light or dolphins performing rhythmic skims and twirls. In these contexts, dancing is a word used as an analogy to describe movement performed for its own sake, especially that which emulates a known dance form such as turning in a waltz, or the forward and back meeting and parting in a folk dance. There is a difference, however, in this use of the word and in its use to describe the purposeful act of dancing a dance.

Similarly, a child's natural spontaneous joy of expressive movement is dancing in an analogous sense only. It is not the art of dance but it certainly forms the basis of it. Just as children need to learn how to write stories and poems, how to create music and how to paint pictures, they also need to learn how to create, perform and appreciate dances.

In one form or another, dance is an established part of primary education in many British schools. Until quite recently, the Laban model, described in the initial pages of chapter 1, was advocated as the most appropriate for primary dance education. Indeed it is still commonly employed to provide dance movement experiences, often guided by radio or television broadcasts. Through such experiences children are seen to be exploring movement in order to express themselves creatively. Conversely, a few schools consider it important to acquaint children with the folk dance heritage of Britain and perhaps of Europe and teach set dances to children. This practice is mostly confined to junior school ages, between seven and eleven years.

In many schools, dance has taken its place as an integral aspect of the primary curriculum, often interrelated with other subjects in theme-based teaching. It has also been seen to be a part of a balanced physical education programme providing expressive movement opportunities in contrast to gymnastic and games activities.

Against this background, there has been a gradual shift towards the art of dance model. In recent years, it has become good practice for pupils in primary schools to experience dance both through creating and performing their own dances and through viewing dances: their own, their peers' and dance works of professional choreographers. Although the terms are different, this three-stranded approach is embodied in the programme of study for dance in the Statutory Order for physical education in the National Curriculum.

Dance in the National Curriculum – key stages 1 and 2

From 1992 dance became a statutory part of Physical Education in the National Curriculum for key stages 1 and 2. Teachers in primary schools are now required to organise dance according to the statutory Programmes of Study (activity specific, dance) which define what pupils should know, understand and be able to do to achieve the End of Key Stage Statements.

Many primary school teachers are in need of further training in order to meet these requirements. In the past decade or so, advisers for physical education and advisory teachers in some counties have provided excellent in-service input for dance in primary schools. However, these posts are disappearing and in-service provision is suffering from a lack of funding.

Teachers who are currently required to teach dance in primary schools will find the comprehensive breakdown of the programmes of study for key stages 1 and 2 in the appendix of this book, to be invaluable. This content for teaching is placed into a theoretical framework in this chapter.

1. The processes of creating, performing and appreciating dances

The National Curriculum Statutory Order describes the three processes for physical education as planning, performing and evaluating. These seem to be synonymous with the processes of creating, performing and appreciating in the *art of dance*. However, there is much debate and confusion about the relationship of the two sets of terms to describe the processes involved. For me, there is a fundamental difference in their meanings, arising from questions of context. In the context of the art of dance participants are creative in making dances, they are engaged in artistic performance when performing dances and they view dances to appreciate them as artistic, aesthetic and cultural phenomena. This is treating dance as an art form. In other kinds of dance experience, e.g. adapting pre-learned traditional folk dance steps into new formations, pupils may well be planning their moves, performing them and then evaluating them in similar ways as they might within a games context.

It has also been argued that in gymnastics pupils make artistic judgements and are concerned with aesthetic qualities too. This may be the case, but aesthetic qualities reside in many aspects of physical education and in myriad ways throughout the curriculum, biology and mathematics for example, so this is not an argument for gymnastics to be singled out and considered an art form in parallel with dance. The art of dance is different in that, like the other art forms of music, poetry, literature, visual arts and drama, it communicates symbolic meaning through a consciously wrought artistic presentation, in this case of movement.

2. The programmes of study for dance for key stages 1 and 2

KEY STAGE 1: DANCE

Pupils should:

experience and develop control, co-ordination, balance, poise and elevation in basic actions including travelling, jumping, turning, gesture, and stillness

explore contrasts of speed, tension, continuity, shape, size, direction, and level and describe what they have done

experience working with a range and variety of contrasting stimuli, including music

be given opportunities to explore moods & feelings through spontaneous responses & through structured tasks

be helped to develop rhythmic responses

experience, and be guided towards making dances with clear beginnings, middles and ends

KEY STAGE 2: DANCE

Pupils should:

make dances with clear beginnings, middles and ends involving improvising, exploring, selecting, and refining content, and sometimes incorporating work from other aspects of the curriculum, in particular music, art and drama

be guided to enrich their movements by varying shape, size, direction, level, speed, tension & continuity

in response to a range of stimuli, express feelings, moods and ideas and create simple characters and narratives in movement

describe and interpret different elements of a dance

DES *Physical Education in the National Curriculum*, April 1992

The programmes of study above are statutory and should be taught in order that end of key stage statements can be reported. The end of key stage statements indicate the skills, knowledge and understanding that should be achieved in physical education overall. Specific reference to skills, knowledge and understanding pertinent to dance is minimal but there are many ways in which they can be implemented through dance. Guidance on application of the dance programmes of study for key stages 1 and 2 will be given later in this chapter. The content of these is reiterated below.

END OF KEY STAGE
STATEMENTS KS1

By the end of the KS pupils should
be able to:

a) plan and perform safely a range
of simple actions & linked movements in response to given tasks &
stimuli

b) practise and improve their
performance

c) describe what they and others
are doing

d) recognise the effects of physical
activity on their bodies

END OF KEY STAGE
STATEMENTS KS2

By the end of the KS pupils should
be able to:

a) plan, practise, improve &
remember more complex sequences
of movement

b) perform effectively in activities
requiring quick decision making

c) respond safely, alone & with
others, to challenging tasks, taking
account of levels of skills and
understanding

d) evaluate how well they & others
perform & behave against criteria
suggested by the teacher and
suggest ways of improving
performance

e) sustain energetic activity over
appropriate periods of time in a
range of physical activities &
understand the effects of exercise
on the body

DES *Physical Education in the National
Curriculum* April 1992

The text below aims to help teachers to interpret the requirements
of the National Curriculum and to demonstrate how the theoretical
basis of the art of dance model in education, described in chapter 1,
can be applied to dance in primary education.

In order to do this, it is necessary to start with the end products
of dance lessons, dances. There are two reasons for this:

a) It is important to consider first what is to be achieved and
learned by the children. What skill, knowledge and understanding
are to be acquired through dance experiences? This is done best
through analysis of potential outcomes of the lesson/s.

b) There is a lack of literature for teachers explaining the ratio-nale, theory and principles behind the practice of completing dance experiences with dances as outcomes in good primary dance teach-ing practice. There are several books available which describe dance content for the primary sector and provide teachers with example lesson plans and tips on how to teach these dance lessons. The latter generally outline the content starting from the beginning warm-up and give an outline of the content of the dance. These texts are good sources for ideas and at least one (*Let's Dance* by Mary Harlow and Linda Rolfe) goes some way towards demonstrating when and how the three processes of creating, performing and appreciating might occur in their sample lessons. The end products, the dances the children will create, perform and appreciate, are not analysed, how-ever. Indeed, no current text examines in detail what is to be learned in dance and through dance from the lesson experiences. It is assumed that if a teacher presents a well-planned lesson out of the text, he/she will learn by example and will be able to plan future lessons.

A dance outcome

The following description of a teacher-created dance framework is intended to provide the reader with an imaginary picture of a new group of year 3 pupils performing the dance outcome at the end of maybe two lessons. A teacher-created dance framework is a composed structure for a dance denoting what kind of movement the children will be doing in each section, the order of the sections and how these relate to make a whole dance. The children fill in the detail of the movement content in their own way. Each part of the dance will be interpreted differently by each pupil, each pair or each group. A well-made teacher-created dance framework has a clear beginning, middle and end, contains variety and contrast, develops logically and achieves coherence of form.

Lesson content leading to the finished performance of this dance outcome based on the teacher-created framework below can be found in the appendix pages 190–5.

DANCE TITLE *Dancing in the Rain in New Wellies*

INTRODUCTION (approximately 16 bars of walking pace music)
Sitting on the floor – pull on to feet imaginary wellington boots.
Admire them, still sitting and/or standing up. Take weight on
different parts of the feet – heels, toes, outside edges, and look at
them. Also lift up one foot at a time to look at parts of the boots,
inside the boot, outside, bottom, heels and toes, etc.

SECTION 1 (approximately 16 bars of skipping rhythm music)
Perform high knee movements (skips, marches, gallops, hops, etc.,
with knees coming up high to 'show off' boots). Do these movements anywhere in the room.

SECTION 2 (approximately 32 bars of lively skipping rhythm music)
Perform the movements of running through, jumping into, kicking
and splashing in puddles.

SECTION 3 (approximately 32 bars of lively travelling and leaping
music)
    In pairs using follow-my-leader and side-by-side relationship
variations, perform a sequence of travelling and leaping movements
in unison.

SECTION 4 (approximately 16 bars of walking rhythm music)
Individually, perform walking and spinning movements playing at
taking weight on different parts of the imaginary wellies, to arrive
back on the spot where the boots were 'put on'.

CONCLUSION (end of last phrase of music above)
Take off wellies and finish in a position looking at them.
    Resources used during the lesson/s include the music and the
video snippet of Gene Kelly performing *Singing in the Rain* from
the film.

Ways in which the above dance outcome implements the programme of study for dance in key stage 1

(The words/phrases taken out of the programme of study are typeset in italic).

• There is emphasis on developing *control* and *balance* in the introduction and section 4 when the children are taking weight on

different parts of their feet, spinning and lifting up one leg to look at the boots. The children should show awareness of use of a range of parts of their feet and use control and balance in demonstrating this range, for example, balancing on toes whilst looking back to see the heels.

• There is *co-ordination* demanded in the above and in all the *travelling* movements, especially in constantly changing moves in section 2 and linking them into the sequence in section 3.

• *Elevation* is obviously emphasised in sections 2 and 3.

• *Travelling* is an emphasised action in this dance. Children should demonstrate a range of travelling steps including walking, marching, running, skipping, galloping, hopping, jumping, etc.

• *Jumping* is also an emphasised action. However, in section 2 the children are jumping in the puddles and in section 3 they are leaping over the puddles. They should show the differences and be able to perform a variety of both kinds of jumping action, i.e. for the jumping into puddles they might use two to two feet jumps, one to two feet jumps, hops, springs from one foot to the other. For section 3 they should show different kinds of travelling leap over the puddles, for example, from one to the other foot, one to both.

• *Level* is mentioned in terms of knees *high* but it is not an emphasised aspect.

• *Music* is used and *rhythmic responses* to it should be apparent in the actions danced. The children should also show awareness of pattern in the music. The structure of phrases/sections and the whole piece will enhance the sense of form and pattern in the dance.

• Through *structured tasks* children will *respond spontaneously* in exploring the *mood* of playfulness in rainy weather (*the stimulus*) throughout the content of the dance.

• The structure of the dance with a clear *beginning, middle* and *end* provides the children with experience of a formed whole. They should show their understanding of this in their performance which should show a readiness to start, a continuity of progression through the dance with some sense of phrasing, and a good held *ending*.

Ways in which the above dance outcome implements the end of key stage statements for physical education in key stage 1

Statement a) The children will be involved in *creating* (*planning*) improvised movement *responses* in the introduction, sections 1, 2, 4 and the conclusion. To do this they will need to select appropriate moves from the range which will have been explored during the lesson/s. They will also have *created* a sequence for section 3 with a partner. This involves appropriate selection and *linking* of movements *in response to the task*. In their performance the children show awareness of the *safety* involved in jumping and landing well and moving freely without bumping into each other.

Statement b) The children will *practise and improve their performance* every time they repeat the dance or sections of it. In particular they will practise their sequences in section 3 of the dance so that they can dance effectively with their partner and with the music and be able to repeat the sequences. The children should also show improvement in their performance through understanding and being inspired by (c) below.

Statement c) The children will be able to *describe what they and others are doing* in the context of watching each other perform. Such performances should include demonstrations of particularly imaginative, original responses to the guided exploration tasks (as in the introduction). Observation tasks can be set when half the class watches the other half and children should also be able to use qualitative language to describe Gene Kelly's actions in the dance *Singing in the Rain*.

Statement d) The children will *recognise the effects of physical activity on their bodies* throughout the lesson/s particularly, of course, in the travelling and jumping activities. The extended exploration of movements for sections 2 and 3 should be spaced sensibly by the teacher. Note that the order of the dance does not have to determine the order of the lesson content. Throughout the explorations and practices of the movements for these sections in the dance, the teacher should help the children aim for *good technique* in taking off from and returning to the ground. This reiterates the *safety* aspect in (a) above. Children should show ability to *apply full energy* in the parts of the dance which require it and should 'save' themselves in other parts. This shows *control and awareness of stamina*.

Ways in which the above dance outcome implements the theoretical basis of the midway model

Clearly, the children will be experiencing the art form of dance and will be involved in creating, performing and appreciating the dance outcome. They should report to parents or others who might ask them that they made a dance about dancing in the rain in new wellies. They may also be able to write or talk about the movements they used, in language similar to that with which they discussed each other's work and the video. This will indicate something about how the experience has influenced their aesthetic and artistic development.

Emphasis on the *midway* model through this dance can clearly be exemplified. The following text is presented in order of the table on page 26 in chapter 1.

1. Equal emphasis on process and on product

The dance outcome or product is a qualitative whole in the sense that it is unified with a clear beginning, middle and end, has contrasting sections, progresses logically and contains a variety of expressive content. The processes towards achieving this end should also have been rich experiences. The children will have been engaged in exploring content for the introduction of the dance, for example, by responding spontaneously to the stimulus and to the teacher's structured tasks as illustrated below:

Extract from lesson plan

TASK – improvise freely in response to stimulus

a) Discussion with children of the idea of having a new pair of wellington boots and playing in the rain.

b) Discussion of the kinds of movements the children might use to examine and admire their boots.

The teacher should have in mind a range of possibilities and feed them in if necessary, but most children will come up with a full range of responses.

c) Improvise the introduction to the music.

The teacher could comment on the original ideas and range of ideas observed in order to improve variety and quality in all the pupils' responses. Some demonstrations would also develop their responses.

TASK – with your partner create a sequence of running and leaping over imaginary puddles.

a) Practise running and leaping individually.

The teacher should remind pupils of the different kinds of leaps they already have in their vocabulary, possibly by asking appropriate questions. The children should select and practise a range of leaps.

b) Practise two ways of working with a partner.

The teacher should set the task of children working in pairs, one of them the leader, the follower copying the leader's run and leaping action in canon. The children should then select one kind of run and leap and practise performing it side by side in unison.

c) Combine the leading and following sequence, the children taking turns and then performing in unison. The following structure may help:

A run and leap B follows copying
B "   "   "   A   "   "
Repeat with different leaps
A and B run and leap together with 2 different leaps.

This is a tightly structured task but it requires the children to select, refine and practise movements in their own ways. In a disciplined way, they are choreographing, making decisions, remembering and repeating the outcome of their exploration.

In the above examples, then, there is equal emphasis on process and product.

2. Equal emphasis on creativity, imagination and individuality, and on acquisition of knowledge of theatre dance

Exploration of content for section 2 of the dance above might progress on the following lines:

TASK – perform the movements of running through, jumping into, kicking and splashing in puddles. A breakdown follows:

a) Set imaginary situation. 'The floor is covered with puddles and you have your new wellington boots on. Show me what you would do.'

b)Either through pupils demonstrating or through the teacher commenting with praise, take some ideas from observation of the children's improvisation in (a) and ask all the children to practise them – for example, running keeping the feet very close and almost skating over the ground; jumping onto two feet with an emphasis on making a big flat-footed splash; kicking with the inside edges of the feet; perform stamping movements walking in a circle within the confines of a large puddle.

c) Watch the video of Gene Kelly's performance of the solo dance and song in *Singing in the Rain*. Discuss the kinds of movements seen and ask the pupils to keep one idea in mind for their own dance.

d) Improvise to the music for section 2 of the dance.

The above progression through a task aiming to achieve a richly expressive and varied response to the stimulus allows for individual creative interpretation. At the same time the children are expanding their own repertoire of appropriate responses by observing and learning from each other, the teacher and, importantly in this art of dance model, from a professional 'ready-made' art work. Hence their creativity and imagination is being educated.

Reference to the professional art work enhances rather than directs their responses. The children cannot copy the movements since they do not have the observation skills to be able to reconstruct what they see (an abundance of movement ideas within the dance) into their own action. What they gain is an impression from a qualitative whole; if asked to recall just one movement idea from the video, it is more than likely to be reproduced in outline only. However, it is always surprising how much the experience of viewing a professional dance work of this nature inspires the children's own creativity. Somehow, many ideas are triggered off in their imaginations when inspired by originality and excellence in examples on the same or similar themes. Young children are particularly receptive to qualitative examples. They take in much more than they can find words to describe and it is often the case that they find it easier to express such impressions through movement than any other medium. Experienced teachers will note nuances of expression, glimmerings of the content and form of the professional art work in the children's own dances. However, each child is triggered by this inspiration in his or her own particular way. Whatever the strength of the impression made by the art work, the dance outcome is entirely derived from each child's own interpretation.

In this way, more often than not subconsciously, the children are developing their creativity, imagination and individuality. At the same time, however, they are learning from the public art world what constitutes originality in imagination and creativity in dance choreography. They are also adding to their own repertoire of an expressive dance vocabulary and are possibly noting ways in which movements can be linked in phrases, contrasted and highlighted. Through reference to a professional art work the pupils are learning more about the techniques of dance. Equal emphasis is thereby put on developing creativity, imagination and individuality, and on acquiring knowledge of theatre dance.

3. Equal emphasis on feelings and on training

It should be clear to the reader that if the task outlined above for section 2 of the dance is delivered as indicated, the children's own feelings will certainly enter into the dance outcome. When discussion takes place, when imaginary situations are explored, when children are watching each other's dances and/or the professional example, they will have feelings about what they see. They will laugh and enjoy the part where Gene Kelly 'goes over the top' in splashing, 'splatting' his feet in the water, kicking and spinning with his umbrella out in front of him. They will also laugh and enjoy the moment when the policeman comes by and Kelly gently shakes the water from his feet and pretends to act normally. This engagement with the art work is a feeling response.

The pupils will imaginatively put such feelings into their own performances and choreographic problem solving, and the process may be regarded as an expression of the child's developing intuition – that is, knowledge absorbed through experience and then emerging in the creative form accompanied by a feeling of 'rightness'. Reid (1983) describes 'illuminated intuition' as that which is fed by direct experience but emerges from the subconscious as inspirational feeling responses to creative tasks.

The marriage of these feeling responses to the acquisition of techniques and knowledge of the subject of dance is difficult to achieve but is nonetheless a necessary objective. Throughout the experiences involved in working on *Dancing in the Rain in New Wellies* pupils will acquire varied knowledge of dance. From creating dances they will learn what is appropriate vocabulary, how to make phrases, how to colour their actions to express and project the meanings. Rather than accepting anything the children produce, the teacher will need to guide pupils who produce inappropriate responses and help them to discriminate and evaluate what they produce in creative work. Gradually pupils should become aware of criteria of appropriateness and originality, even though they may be unable to understand these terms.

The children should also learn how to improve their performances. The teacher will need to direct the pupils' attention to performance qualities so that they consciously think about and work on, for example, extra stretch, extra height and extra resilience in jumping actions. A few moments in each lesson directed towards such objectives will gradually increase the children's dance performance skills. Although there should not be an emphasis on technical training and acquisition of practical dance skills at primary level, it is important to keep in mind the fact that children who have some skill can express in a feelingful way better than those without such skills.

Keeping a balance between subjective feelings, on the one hand, and the knowledge to be learned and/or skills to be practised, on the other, is a necessary aspect of the *midway* art of dance in education model. The above example illustrates how this might occur but, of course, each dance experience varies in the manner in which such an objective is achieved.

4. Equal emphasis on movement principles and on stylised techniques

The dance outcome of *Dancing in the Rain in New Wellies* is almost entirely derived from the movement principles outlined by Laban. The simple basis of these principles is easy to grasp in that every movement we perform in daily life can be described under the four headings of action, dynamics, space and relationship: what the body is doing, how it is doing it in terms of time, energy and continuity, where the body is moving in space and how the movement relates to objects and/or people. The non-specialised terms used to describe movement content make this set of principles accessible to teachers without knowledge of dance. The dance outcome described on page 52 demonstrates how the principles can be used as a framework within which the teacher will set creative tasks.

The difficulty of using general movement principles rather than prescribed vocabulary lies in the lack of criteria to guide the teacher on the range of content appropriate for different age groups within each concept. For example, just what sort and how many different travelling actions is an eight-year-old capable of performing? It is also difficult for the teacher to know what constitutes good dance movement. For example, what does a dance leap look like as opposed to an everyday leap over a puddle?

Lack of a defined vocabulary of dance movements also poses problems in that any progression made has to be determined by the teacher. If, for example, the children have previously explored taking weight onto different parts of the feet in other dance contexts, the teacher would expect some development in their abilities to perform the task in the introduction of the dance described here. They would need less guidance in their exploration and they should produce a greater range of answers to the task because they are applying known vocabulary to a different situation. Of course each new situation should produce new and different movement outcomes when exploring content, because the idea is different. So although the children may have experienced all five of the basic jumps which answers the task of jumping into imaginary puddles in section 2 of the dance, the qualities/dynamics and even the look and feel of the jumps will be quite different for this particular dance – jumping *into* concentrates more on the landing than on the flight, uses the arms differently and the focus is perhaps down rather than up.

The DES statutory guidelines are not much help in this context. Progression is only cursorily built into the programme of study for dance, and statements such as

> be given opportunities to increase the range and complexity of body actions, including step patterns and use of body parts.
>
> (Key Stage 2)

are open to many interpretations. What degree of complexity can we expect of this age group? What constitutes a more complex step pattern?

Later in this chapter on primary dance education some help is given on the problems of using the somewhat open set of movement principles defined by Laban as content for dance education. For the present, let us now concentrate on positive aspects of the principles as a basis for the dance outcome, *Dancing in the Rain in New Wellies.*

One important benefit of using movement principles rather than set steps to be learned and practised lies in their flexibility as a means of encouraging creative responses. To set a task of 'taking weight on different parts of the feet' limits the children to a type of movement but allows freedom of choice within the type. For instance, the children will all be answering the task in taking weight on different parts of their feet but each will be performing individual versions of doing this. At any one moment, a range of different parts of the feet bearing weight, toes, heels, inside edges, flat feet, one ball of foot and one heel successively, etc., should be evident. The principles therefore constitute a template with which the pupils find their own dance movement vocabulary.

Another benefit of Laban's movement principles for the primary stage in education has to be the fact that the content and terms for dance movement are derived from everyday movement and everyday descriptive words. This makes it possible for all to be able to create and perform dances immediately because we all have an everyday movement repertoire even if physically disabled in some way and we understand the simple terms used to describe such movements. However, although this may well be a valid starting point for children and adult beginners in dance, there should be a shift away from what can be discerned as everyday action towards that which can be described as the art of dance in the public sense.

The art of dancing, as made clear at the beginning of this chapter, is not a natural activity. There is much to learn in order that the natural everyday actions can be transformed into dance movement. Defined techniques such as ballet and the Graham or Cunningham techniques are means towards this end but none of the classical or contemporary dance techniques is suitable for primary education. So how does the teacher work on an everyday movement vocabulary and make the result look like dance? The answer lies in stylisation and technical refinement of movement. Primary teachers need to learn how to achieve these.

To achieve stylisation, it is often the case that everyday movements are exaggerated. For example, the high knee movements in section 1 of the *Dancing in the Rain in New Wellies* dance will be as high and large as possible, and to emphasise the reason for the movements (to show off boots) the children should be encouraged to emphasise different parts of the leg or foot in focus – for example, knees-high skipping actions with the legs turned out so that the inside of the boots can be seen or knees-high marches with the toes turned up so that the toes of the wellies can be looked at while marching. Such emphases change everyday skipping or marching movements for the purposes of the dance. Any addition of arm or head movements would elaborate the actions even further. Also taking the movements in directions other than forwards – backwards, round in small circles, or sideways with legs turned out (crossing in front and behind perhaps), adds an enhanced spatial patterning.

Giving actions a rhythmic pattern also makes an everyday movement into dance. The children's use of the beat and accents in the music should provide a rhythmic structure and gradually they should be able to link movements into phrases appropriately punctuated with pauses and stillness. This means that in section 1 of the dance the high knee movements will change in some way at the beginning of phrases and will be performed rhythmically to the music, thus colouring the movement with accents, pauses and stops. Stylisation, then, can be achieved through exaggeration, elaboration and rhythmic structuring of everyday action. However, it still may not look like dance movement until it has been technically refined.

To achieve technical refinement of all dance movement and to look like a professional dancer take many years of dedicated practice. At the primary level this aspect of the art of dance model should not be emphasised, yet there are definite merits in striving for sufficient technical competence so that children feel proud and confident in their performances. Without exception the many hundreds of primary children I have taught enjoyed improving their physical skills in dance. Simple exercises to improve their use of feet in skipping, for example, were practised in the playground and in the dance hall before the lesson commenced. These may include:

a) sitting on the floor, legs extended and knees straight, to enable the child to flex and extend the ankles and toes. Greater sensitivity and control can be achieved if the children are able to isolate the movements of the toes and ankles as well as incorporating both parts in full extension. Exercise a) may be followed by b), c) and d).

b) toes and heels gently touching the floor while in a sitting position with knees bent.

c) standing up, feet alternately pulling out of imaginary treacle on the floor, heels first and toes last.

d) marching, pushing the floor away with each foot lift.

All four of these exercises concentrate attention on the child learning how to extend ankles and toes fully whilst skipping. Eventually the children will skip with beautifully stretched or pointed feet and this skill can be transferred to other actions such as jumping, leaping and any movements lifting feet from the floor.

There are many ways of improving technical skills in dance actions and generally teachers will learn these from experience or courses. All teachers, however, have the ability to improve the qualities in their children's performances. For example, the lively and energetic qualities needed for section 3 of the dance under scrutiny here can be improved through the use of imagery, through the teacher's encouragement of pupils who show the desired qualities, through use of the video resource and discussion of what makes Gene Kelly's performance lively. There are many ways of improving the dynamic colouring of the children's movements. Also body shape and use of space are easily observed by the teacher. Comments on such spatial aspects which are not necessarily visible to the children will improve their work.

Above all, if children achieve expressive clarity in their dances they will be more likely to master the technical aspects of the movements. For example, a child might choose to perform section 4 of the dance with walking into spinning on toes and rocking back to heels to look at the boots and then sinking while turning into a sitting position. This is quite a complex sequence demanding smooth linking of actions and control in balance. If the child is thoroughly engaged in the expressive intention, however, it is likely that repetition and practice of the sequence to get the meaning across will develop technical competence to enable the child to perform it well. Of course, given the option, it is unlikely that the child will choose movements too difficult to perform, and progressively more difficult demands need to be built into the framework of future tasks so that children do not perform the same movements over and over again in different contexts, never progressing. Teachers should be aware of this danger when using general movement principles and make the tasks progressively more challenging, especially for the most able. Of course, the advantage of movement principles over a set vocabulary of content for dance must lie in the fact that interpretation of tasks (such as that set for section 4 of the dance) can be at different levels according to the ability of individual children.

In this art of dance model for primary schools then, there should be more emphasis on movement principles but with attention given to stylisation and technical refinement of everyday movement. In this way children will absorb an art of dance vocabulary.

5 . Equal emphasis on problem solving approach and on directed teaching

Although at primary school level there should be more emphasis on the open-ended problem-solving approach than on didactic teaching methods, in this art of dance model there should be some learning directly from the teacher or from professional dancers.

The dance outcome *Dancing in the Rain in New Wellies* is almost totally derived from the problem-solving approach in that the pupils have explored and selected movement content for themselves in responding to the tasks. However, there are degrees of freedom for the children when problem solving: in the introduction, for example, pupils explore movement in response to the idea of having new wellies and admiring them. The discussion serves only as a stimulus for the children's imaginations and the teacher is not suggesting movement content in any way, one is simply drawing it out from the pupils by talking about the kinds of things they might do in the situation. The teacher, in this way, acts as catalyst and guide and the pupils learn from each other as well as discovering for themselves through experimenting with the idea in the creative situation.

An alternative problem-solving approach is used in section 2 of the dance framework. Here, as indicated in the breakdown of the task on page 56, the pupils start with a very open task and then possibly, through practice of specified movements selected by the teacher, through observation and demonstration by one or two pupils and by taking in outline a movement idea from the video, they are directed to expand their own vocabulary with ideas from other sources. The art of dance in education model aims for a constant shift from open to closed tasks, with much of the teaching being *midway* between the two.

Even for 7–8 year old pupils it is possible to discern different degrees of teacher intervention/pupil directed learning in the dance framework. The introduction, sections 1, 2 and 4 allow for greater degrees of individual interpretation of the task than section 3. The latter section could be tightened up considerably if it is taught in the way described on pages 55–6. Here, the teacher is directing the order of the movement phrases and the pattern of the partner work. This is not totally directed in that the children still choose the travel and leap actions they are going to use, but it limits their input to this choice only.

Most dance lessons should contain some directed teacher input so that pupils are stretched beyond their own capacities some of the time. This directed teacher input can be disguised, though, in that there are several occasions in creative dance lessons where the teacher selects a child to demonstrate a movement idea and then, as indicated above, says, 'Let us all try that movement.' In this way the teacher is requiring all the pupils to experience a way of moving determined by someone other than themselves. This subtle directed teaching approach may well be used with a resource such as *Singing in the Rain* though, in the dance outcome described, it is used for inspiration only. For older children the teacher could have taken a sequence from Gene Kelly's dance and replicated it fairly exactly as a section in the children's dance.

6. Artistic education

a) Understanding what a dance is

The intention of a dance outcome is to convey meaning to an audience, and this immediately puts the experience into an artistic context. Pupils gain further insight into the nature of dances as artefacts, each having unique content and form. At this stage, the teacher will create the structures of most of the dances and these will be simple and conventional with beginnings, middles and ends. These structures are frameworks within which the pupils create their own movement contents. This framework approach provides the teacher with the means of extending the pupils' perceptions of what constitutes a dance by their experience of increasingly complex dance structures. The dance *Dancing in the Rain in New Wellies* is a much more developed form than the *Balloon Dance* (see page 202). The former has an introduction and conclusion with four sections between them and lasts for about two minutes, the latter has a beginning, middle and ending phrases and lasts for about a minute. Hence between the beginning of the National Curriculum dance experience at five years old to the beginning of year 3 (the end of key stage 1), the children's perceptions of what constitutes a dance has developed considerably.

Creating structures for dances is difficult, however, since the process incorporates shaping movement within given confines of time and space. It is therefore strongly recommended that most of the dance outcomes are structured by the teacher, though, sometimes, through discussion with the children, the dance structure can be created during the lesson. Also, occasionally by the end of key stage 1 and more often by the end of key stage 2, pupils should be able to create simple dance structures for themselves. These are easier for them if they use ready-made forms as templates: poems, music, stories, for example.

The knowledge and understanding put into practice here will have been gained intuitively for the most part in that the children will gain a sense of form from experience of the teacher's 'well-made' dance structures. More discussion of this point will follow later but, as with learning from 'ready-mades' in poetry, literature, music, and drama, there is much that enters the child's awareness without a conscious learning of facts or techniques.

b) Skills, knowledge and understanding gained through the processes of performing, creating and appreciating dances

The skills listed on pages 30–1 will all be addressed to some extent in the description of the dance *Dancing in the Rain in New Wellies.*

Performing

Under the heading of 'performing', the children will develop further their physical skills in travelling, jumping, leaping and balancing on, and isolating parts of, their feet. They will practise linking the movements into phrases and how to punctuate these phrases with pauses and stops. They will practise performance of a range of dynamic qualities – a slow, quiet beginning and end contrasted with a very energetic leaping climax in section 3. They will share the overall space and show awareness of shaping space as a means of expressing the idea, for example leaping over puddles. They will practise dancing rhythmically to the music and presenting the theme expressively. In the partner sequence they will learn to dance in unison and canon, adapting and fitting in with each other.

Creating

Under the heading of 'creating dances' the children will learn more about exploration and selection of content appropriate to a theme. They will discover new actions coloured in different ways by the rhythmic, dynamic, spatial and relationship features suited to expression of the idea. They will learn more about features in music and the use of them to enhance expression of the idea – for example, the bouncy quality for section 2 of the dance, the energy and phrasing in section 3 which should be matched in the pairs' work of running and leaping movements. They will learn to be discriminating in their choice of content through seeking original outcomes rather than easy answers in their own explorations. Their creative abilities will also be enhanced through taking imaginative leaps in response to watching each other or the video clip. They will gain some understanding of the discipline of creating phrases, remembering them and being able to repeat them. They will add to their growing intuitive understanding of form and they will select movements/stillnesses to show awareness of the beginning, middle and end of the dance and its sections. Finally, in presenting the dance outcome, they should show an awareness of its expressive intention and how this may be communicated to the audience. They should also be able to comment on the difference of genre between their dances and the video example. Gene Kelly's dance is essentially a tap dance and, therefore, some of the movements are derived from a specific tap vocabulary. Nonetheless there are several movements – for example, the on and off the pavement steps and the cross-over grapevine step – which are universally applicable in Western dance forms. This awareness of style/genre is important in learning how to create dances.

Viewing

Children should observe all the above aspects in their own dance, in the dances of peers and in the video example. They should be able to describe the content using the appropriate terminology (for example, a jump from one foot to two feet) and use some qualitative words to describe the dynamics and expressive aspects in what they see – for example, the indulgent deceleration in Gene Kelly's leap onto and lean from the lamp post. The children will readily ascribe meanings to particular movements but they should listen to what others say and learn that a range of meanings is legitimate in this context.

Pupils should gain experience in evaluating their own dances and those of their peers. When viewing dances, improvisations or phrases, teachers should always give children something to look for and then question them on those specific aspects. If children are asked to criticise what they see they should learn, through the teacher's example, to be constructive. For instance, in viewing a small group performing section 1, the teacher could ask the pupils to notice any unusual responses and ask them to say why they think the responses are unusual. Children are usually good at doing this and if, for example, a child were picked out for lifting the knees high out sideways and turning the foot up and inwards to view the sole of the wellington boot, the teacher could praise both the viewer and the performer for responding well to the task. In this way children learn that guided viewing of a dance is as much a part of the dance education learning process as the physical activities of creating and performing dances.

Appreciation

Through the above processes – performing, creating and viewing the parts and the whole dance – pupils will develop appreciation of artistic aspects of their own and others' work.

7. Aesthetic education

In all the performing, creating and viewing experiences involved in producing the dance outcome *Dancing in the Rain in New Wellies*, the children should be encouraged to perceive the feelings embodied in the movements. They should practise performing to gain a kinesthetic feeling of the sensory qualities: for example, in section 2 of the dance, bounciness denotes expressive qualities of carefree happy enjoyment, a sense of well-being, etc. In most instances talking about their kinesthetic feelings and perceptions of aesthetic sensory and expressive qualities will help children to become more aware of them. It is important, therefore, that the teacher plans for such talk and encourages the children to use analogy and metaphor in describing what they feel – for example, with reference to section 2, 'it feels like being on a trampoline'.

There are a great many opportunities to develop perceptions of sensory, expressive and formal qualities in the dance performed by Gene Kelly. The contrast between the exuberant kicking and jumping into the river of rain followed by his suddenly stopping and quietly explaining 'I'm singing and I'm dancing in the rain' to the policemen can be seen as a climax of the dance. There are definite sections in the dance and each phrase has a beginning, middle and end. The introduction and conclusion of the dance are very good examples for discussion and should be compared by the children with their own dances.

Much talk about the video clip will help the children see more and gain more enjoyment each time they see it. This will gradually heighten the children's sensitivity to the aesthetic qualities of that dance.

8. Cultural education

a) Conceptions of the nature of dance and dances
The idea of a dance symbolically communicating enjoyment of rainy weather (expression) and its structure in relation to time (form) derive from the Western tradition of what constitutes a dance. Experience of such dance outcomes will therefore reinforce these concepts. Moreover, the vocabulary derived from an everyday experience of playing in rain has comic undertones in that it is not customary to enjoy the rain in countries that have so much of it! Rain carries a different meaning in hot desert places. Gene Kelly communicates his elation very clearly and the incredulity expressed by

others conveys this message even more clearly. Some of the signs and symptoms conveyed in the dance are therefore culturally bound but others have universal meanings – the sense of happiness conveyed through bouncy skipping and jumping actions, for example. However, even though the movements within the dance may have universal meanings, the way that they are abstracted from everyday contexts and exaggerated through extra extension, rhythmical and dynamic patterning is not a universal approach to dance composition. This is essentially a Western approach to choreography.

The video could be compared and contrasted with an African or Aboriginal tribal rain dance which has very different intentions: not to entertain and communicate artistically, but to perform a ritual of prayer for rain or a celebration of it. The children should easily see the differences in the movement and messages conveyed. In the tribal dances the focus is generally inward within the group and not outward to an audience and there is no emphasis on the skill of the dancers as performers. Rather the emphasis is on the strength of the collective need for, and joy in, rain for the growth of crops.

b) Understanding of types of dance (genre) and styles
The dance on video is a mixture of tap and stage musical dancing styles. The children should appreciate this genre as typical of musical films made in the 1950s. They may benefit from seeing other dances from the same film, especially *Make them Laugh*, to see how gymnastics and slapstick entered into a tap dance to make it spectacular and comic. This brief historical glimpse gives some background to the study of the art of dance in the theatre.

Comparison of the *Singing in the Rain* dance with their own dances will provide the children with a concept of genre and style in that clearly their dances cannot be called tap or stage dances. Stylisation is not a main focus in this dance but opportunities should be taken to introduce the concept during key stages 1 and 2 so that an understanding of it develops gradually and can be demonstrated by the end of key stage 3.

Experience of creating their own dances in a particular style, such as a Chinese dragon dance or African drumming dance, at the same time as studying the real things, will help children appreciate that different cultures produce different dance forms and styles. This is an important aspect of the art of dance in education which should encourage awareness of cultural diversity.

RESOURCE-BASED TEACHING/LEARNING AND CROSS CURRICULAR LINKS

Using *Singing in the Rain* as a resource has proved to be helpful in encouraging the children's enthusiasm, their production of ideas during lessons and their final performance; it is also a means of teaching children to analyse dance styles and their own feeling responses. This resource, therefore, acts as a good exemplar in artistic and aesthetic terms and, as indicated above, it can also be used to inform children about implicit cultural features of dances.

Viewing tasks

In the dance experiences discussed above, however, the resource *Singing in the Rain* is not a central focus. It should affect and guide the variety and quality of the movement content rather than become its source. The teacher would need to decide when and how it should first be introduced but is strongly advised not to show it at the start of the project. The video snippet should be shown first when the children are exploring content for section 2 of *Dancing in the Rain in New Wellies*, either at the end of lesson 1 or during lesson 2. It is important that viewing tasks are built into lessons as progressive elements which in some way push the children on in their learning. They are not meant to be entertaining interludes! The task leading up to section 2 of the dance outcome (see page 56) shows that the children's own exploratory improvisations precede their viewing of the video, which is used to extend their own ideas in response to the task.

If this is the very first time the video has been seen the viewing tasks might be structured as follows:

a) view the whole of the dance from the moment Kelly says goodbye to the lady.

Questions to encourage discussion:

'Why do you think he dances and sings in the rain?'

'How do you know he is happy?'

'Which movements do you remember best?'

b) watch the part of the dance between the sung sections (nearly the whole of it!) and remember some of the movements which you really like – perhaps those which make you laugh.

Questions to encourage discussion:

'Which was your favourite movement and why have you chosen it?'

With one of the childrens' choices in mind, 'Can we put some words on the board to describe it?' (For example, the flat-footed two to two feet jumps in the large puddle; words or phrases such as splat, splash, hit, smash, making frog-like jumps, large bounces as on a trampoline.)

'Is this the biggest splashing movement he performs?'

'Are there some other big movements you remember?'

'Are there any small or quiet movements?'

Such questions guide and limit the pupils' viewing of the piece but at the same time require them to view, recall and describe particular movements in more detail than in the first viewing task.

Performing tasks

Following the viewing tasks above, the children could be asked to remember a splashing movement they liked in the film and to prac-tise performing it for their own dance. As made clear in chapter 1, it is unlikely that they would be able to copy the movement exactly, nor should this be the aim. Rather, the essence of it should be captured and the teacher should encourage the children to put energy and expression into it, using Gene Kelly as a qualitative example. This kind of referencing in respect of quality and expres-sion in performance could occur about twice in the lessons leading towards the dance outcome. Teachers could concentrate attention on the stretch and resilience in Kelly's movements, on the changes of quality from strong and energetic to soft and small, on the rhythm and phrasing (sentences) in his dance. These are just a few of the qualities which could improve the pupils' performances.

Creating tasks

The above viewing tasks could and should lead into creative tasks. The selection and refinement of their favourite splashing movement from the film for their own dance need to be thought about in terms of juxtaposition with other movements. The children would need to integrate the action into their own 'sentence' of movement and even if it remains improvisation, there has to be some adjustment of what should precede and follow it.

This may be the closest they get to using actual movements out of the video. The resource will serve creative ends through feeding the children's intuitive grasp of the artistic and aesthetic qualities of the dance. For example, they will gain a sense of expressive variety and form through perceiving the range of movements and expressive ideas in the piece. Its overall structure of beginning, middle and end, each part having contrasts and climaxes, will contribute to a growing sense of form and its artistic purpose. Children will gain this sense through perceiving and feeling the coherence of the piece; it does not have to be pointed out to them. Indeed, these concepts are probably too abstract for this age group to grasp. Nevertheless, as suggested above and in chapter 1 of this book, a good deal of 'rubbing off' may occur and this in turn will enrich the children's creative work in dance.

Cultural/historical tasks

Some discussion of these has already taken place under the heading of artistic education. Clearly the visual/audio resource of the filmed dance helps the children to see what tap dance looks and sounds like. They should also be able to make comment on the time and context in which the film is set, i.e. a musical set in the 1930s/40s and about Hollywood show business. In addition, it is worth taking the opportunity to discuss the Western attitudes towards rain, and, if the opportunity arises, comparing this film with one about tribal rain dance/s, which can only develop further the pupils' awareness of cultural diversity.

Cross curriculum links

Most primary dance experiences are linked into thematic or project teaching schemes, so that the aims for dance extend further than the boundaries of the subject itself.

The medium of dance can enhance and reinforce other forms of knowledge, understanding and skills. For example, meaningful language work can be undertaken by children, such as finding words to describe movements and feelings about them, studying rhymes in the song *Singing in the Rain* and perhaps writing poems about their own dances, and writing stories that relate to their own dance or to the video exemplar; there are opportunities to explore musical concepts by looking at the structure of phrases and perceiving the dynamic, expressive and formal qualities of these; and, as we have seen, it is possible to learn about different cultures in various ways.

Conclusion

This chapter on the art of dance in primary schools illustrates how the National Curriculum programme of study and end of key stage statements can be addressed through understanding and applying the theoretical basis for the art of dance in education model presented in chapter 1.

The main aim has been to demonstrate the features of the model in detail through scrutiny of one dance outcome and the dance experiences leading up to it. Alternative dance outcomes, experienced at other stages in the primary curriculum, would obviously have been illustrated differently. However, I hope that, having understood the theory behind the practice in this one example, teachers will be able to extend the concepts involved to other examples.

The problem in using a single example only is not so much one of how teachers can relate theory to practice in the context of different dance outcomes, but of how they may translate ideas for dances into qualitative learning experiences. It is one thing to be able to use a theoretical framework to analyse a given dance outcome and its preceding lessons, and quite another to create those outcomes and lesson materials. There is also the problem of making relationships between the different dance experiences when planning a coherent dance curriculum, both within each school year and over the entire primary spectrum.

To these ends, the appendix of this book provides further teacher-created dance frameworks, outlining programmes of study content for lessons. Detailed interpretations of the programmes of study for key stages 1 and 2 provide many more ideas and give guidance concerning progression in dance within primary schools. My aim is that teachers will be able to apply the theoretical concepts discussed here and in chapter 1 to the examples of content in the appendix and those in other texts.

3

The Art of Dance in Secondary Schools

Background – towards a consensus view of dance as art

It is perhaps possible to say that there is little evidence of the older *modern educational dance* approach for dance education in secondary schools today. The shift towards the *midway* model described in chapter 1 has largely taken place because many of the specialist dance teachers entering secondary schools during the past two decades have been trained in this approach and because the GCSE and A level examinations have underpinned and reinforced such changes. Moreover, there has been a much closer liaison between schools and professional dance artists in that the latter have been encouraged to work in education by the Arts Council and Regional Arts Associations. This policy has helped to bridge the gap between dance in schools and dance in the theatre. Visits to the theatre, artists in schools and videos of professional dance work are all important resources for dance programmes in secondary schools today.

In addition to many newly-informed teachers entering the profession, there have been a number of in-service courses for established teachers. Most secondary school dance teachers are, therefore, successfully delivering an art of dance education. However, as indicated in chapter 1 of this book, the changes in practice have pre-empted a thoroughly developed conceptual basis for the art of dance in secondary education. It is important now to identify and examine the rationale and theory behind the practice in order that teachers can be clear about what they are doing in dance education and why they are employing the practices they use most. Knowledge of the theory behind the aims, contents, methodologies and assessment for the art of dance, both within the National

Curriculum and outside it, including the available examination contexts, is a necessity for all teachers of dance if they are to consolidate, develop and extend their practice. The content of this chapter aims to help teachers make theoretical links between chapter 1 of this book and their practice of teaching the art of dance in school.

The dominant model in secondary schools today can be labelled the art of dance in that the three processes of performing, creating and appreciating are employed by most teachers to provide their students with an all-round experience. However, the tried and tested approaches in teaching each strand of the model are in need of development and, above all, of effective integration.

The following text is presented in the same plan as chapter 2 on the art of dance in primary schools. Hence, the dance content of the programme of study for key stages 3 and 4 is examined in relation to the end of key stage statements and this, together with the content of GCSE, AS and A level examinations, is analysed and applied to the theoretical basis for the art of dance in education presented in chapter 1 of this book.

National Curriculum – key stages 3 and 4

The Department of Education and Science document *Physical Education in the National Curriculum* (1992) states that during key stage 3 'pupils should pursue the programmes of study for a minimum of four areas of each activity with games compulsory each year'. In reality, this leaves dance out altogether, particularly for boys unfortunately, and, if it is included, there is little scope for an adequate dance programme within a broad and balanced physical education curriculum. The umbrella subject itself, physical education, is unlikely to achieve more than three lessons a week in the average secondary school, so dance in the National Curriculum will only be delivered for part of each year, if at all.

At key stage 4, the physical education programme is cut down further. Dance is one of a list of many activities from which schools select two. Some areas, however, have more than one activity under their umbrella: games, for example, can include any number of named games, and outdoor and adventure activities can include anything from fishing to climbing. It is permissible to select the two activities from the same area so specialisation in games only, for example, becomes a possibility. Dance on the other hand, judged by the programme of study, seems to limit the activity to the art form. This means that, except for those taking GCSE, it is not possible to specialise in dance alone at key stage 4. This seems to be an anomaly caused by inclusion of dance within the subject heading of physical education.

Before the National Curriculum became statutory – which applied to year 7 in key stage 3 in 1992–1993 and will apply successively to all key stages by 1996 – dance was taught within creative/expressive arts programmes in many secondary schools. Indeed, it is a backward step for the art of dance to have been officially labelled a component of *physical education* in 1992 after years of fighting, since 1944, to achieve recognition for dance as a subject in its own right. In 1993 there are signs already that head teachers and governors no longer wish to appoint specialist teachers of dance but want physical education teachers who can teach dance.

I do not intend here to debate further issues relating to dance within physical education in the National Curriculum since this is not the focus of the book. However, at the time of writing, the future of dance in the state secondary sector of education in the UK does not only look promising. Not only is there little room for dance within physical education but the National Curriculum overall is too extensive for the available hours in the week. There is also pressure from the government to improve science teaching. Something has to give, in an extremely tightly packed and budgeted.National Curriculum programme. No doubt dance and other arts will suffer yet again since they are largely seen as peripheral by many in authority. The battle for dance will continue to be fought by its many dedicated teachers, by some head teachers who believe in its value, and by national organisations such as the National Dance Teachers' Association.

On the more positive side, there is evidence that dance has grown in status over the past two decades and this is acknowledged by the fact that it *is* in the National Curriculum (albeit as an option for key stages 3 and 4) and that there are examinations in dance at GCSE, AS and A levels.

Teachers who are delivering dance within the National Curriculum have much responsibility to retain what has been achieved in much reduced curriculum circumstances. The success of dance within a broad and balanced physical education programme will be due to the application by teachers of what they know to be 'good practice' in dance education to the statutory programmes of study and end of key stage statements. These statements, however, are exceptionally scanty and need to be interpreted. (See the appendix for full clarifications and interpretations of the programmes of study.)

The content in the text below should also help teachers to fill out and interpret the outline statutory orders. Moreover, it will help them to understand how the practice incorporated in the consensus art of dance in education model and its theoretical basis have important roles to play if the statutory orders are to be met effectively and without detriment to the latest developments in teaching the art of dance in education.

The processes of creating, performing and appreciating

As for key stages 1 and 2, the National Curriculum Statutory Order describes three processes for physical education as planning, performing and evaluating. The reader should turn back to page 48 to consider my views on the relationship of these three terms to those employed in the art of dance in education model. As the text below progresses, it should become obvious that at the secondary stage the process of creating shifts towards the discipline of choreography, the process of performing towards the discipline of public performance and appreciating towards critical appreciation of artistic, aesthetic and cultural qualities. Evidence of such knowledge, skills and understanding are expected in a student's practical, verbal and written work. Hence there is perhaps more focus on the *outcomes* of the dance processes and the *discipline* of the art of dance at secondary level.

The processes are important organising principles for the art of dance in education model, and the text below will make constant reference to the activities of creating, performing and appreciating dances. They are considered integral to skills development and a growing knowledge and understanding of the art of dance.

The programmes of study for key stages 3 and 4

KEY STAGE 3: DANCE

Pupils should:
be taught how to develop and use appropriate methods of composition, styles and techniques to communicate meanings and ideas

be guided to create and perform short dances showing sensitivity to the style of accompaniment

be taught to perform set dances, showing an understanding of style

be taught to support their own dance compositions with written and/or oral descriptions of their intentions and outcomes

be taught to describe, analyse, and interpret dances recognising stylistic aspects of production and cultural/historical contexts

KEY STAGE 4: DANCE

Pupils should:
be given opportunities to create dances which successfully communicate the artistic intention.

be taught to perform complex and technically more demanding dances accurately and expressively

be given opportunities to dance in a range of styles showing understanding of form and content

be guided to record the process of composition

be guided to devise and design aspects of production for their own compositions

be given opportunities to describe, interpret and evaluate all aspects of dance including choreography, performance, cultural and historical contexts and production

Physical Education in the National Curriculum (DES April 1992 pp. 9 & 11)

As indicated already these programmes of study are not compulsory except for those schools selecting to offer dance at key stages 3 and 4. In these cases they are statutory and should be taught in order that end of key stage statements can be reported. The end of key stage statements are indicative of the skills, knowledge and understanding to be achieved through the total physical education programme and so they are written in very general terms only. However, as for key stages 1 and 2, there are many ways in which they can be implemented through the dance programmes of study. The end of key stage statements are as follows:

END OF KEY STAGE STATEMENTS KS3	END OF KEY STAGE STATEMENTS KS4
By the end of the KS pupils should be able to:	By the end of the KS pupils should be able to:
a) devise and adapt strategies and tactics across appropriate activities within the programmes of study	a) show increased knowledge, improved competence and safe performance in their selected activities
b) adapt and refine existing skills and develop new skills safely across the activities in the programmes of study	b) understand and take different roles in their selected activities
c) practise and perform movement compositions devised by themselves and others in appropriate activities in the programmes of study	c) develop and apply their own criteria for judging performance
d) understand and evaluate how well they and others have achieved what they set out to do, appreciate strengths and weaknesses and suggest ways of improving	d) prepare, carry out and monitor personal programmes for a healthy and enjoyable lifestyle, considering the use of community resources where appropriate
e) understand the short and long-term effects of exercise on the body systems and decide where to focus their involvement in physical activity for a healthy and enjoyable lifestyle	

Physical Education in the National Curriculum (DES April 1992 pp. 8 & 10)

The following text will interpret the above programmes of study and end of key stage statements for dance in key stages 3 and 4 and demonstrate how the theoretical basis for the art of dance in education, described in chapter 1, can be applied to dance for ages 11–16. The reader is reminded that the focus here is on dance in the National Curriculum. The GCSE Dance examination will be discussed later in this section although all of the content in the National Curriculum programmes of study is implicit in the GCSE syllabus and therefore all that is said about the former is applicable to the latter.

As with discussion of the art of dance in the primary sector, it is necessary to start with the dance outcome. It is just as important for secondary students to come to know and understand dance through experiencing dances as it is for primary pupils. Each lesson, or more frequently each series of lessons, should culminate in a dance outcome which can be repeated, performed and discussed as an art work. Increasingly through key stages 3 and 4 students will have greater autonomy in defining the intention and structuring the choreography and production. By the end of key stage 4 they should be making and performing dances entirely created by themselves. En route, however, they will learn much from the teacher's choreographic, performance and appreciation tasks and from the teacher-created frameworks for compositions which will be employed, particularly during years 7 to 9, to help students structure their dances.

A dance outcome

The following description of a dance derived from a teacher-created dance framework (see chapter 2 page 51) for year 9 pupils will provide an imaginary outcome of three lessons which can be discussed in relation to the National Curriculum programme of study and end of key stage statements for key stage 3. It will also be analysed to demonstrate how the theoretical basis in chapter 1 underpins the art of dance in practice for year 9 pupils.

DANCE TITLE *Pool Idling* (imaginary setting: outdoor pool on holiday in sunny weather)

MUSIC Introduction of *Shine On You Crazy Diamond* (Pink Floyd) from *Fame – A Collection of Great Dance Songs*

INTRODUCTION (music, the first section prior to solo flute sound coming in)

A few pupils at a time enter slowly and dreamily and at random from edges of the room to own spot (all facing one direction), move slowly into different positions (lying, sitting, kneeling, standing) and stare dreamily into space watching imaginary people in the pool, perhaps doodling with hands or feet.

SECTION 1 (music, the first section up to the first solo guitar lead)
Stretch out into a lying position on backs, arms above heads. From this starting position create a solo sequence of motifs incorporating arching, curling, stretching, rocking and rolling movements, giving an illusion of being in water, floating in it gently and slowly. Keep in contact with the floor most of the time but use one rising and falling action during the sequence.

SECTION 2 (music, the section up to the accented guitar lead)
Move to partner and perform motifs, including assisted jumps, movements onto and sliding off partner, through, under and round partner, lifting and lowering partner. All of these movements should be performed in slow motion as if playing around in water.

Transition (music, between the above section and the next prior to drum beats)

At clapped hands signal all run as if through water to make groups of four.

SECTION 3 (the sequence music leading up to the words)
In the group of four, choreograph a sequence in unison with one incidence of canon and employing at least one swimming action out of the video *Waterless Method of Swimming Instruction*. The sequence should suggest receiving imaginary instructions from the side of the pool to improve swimming strokes.

CONCLUSION (the introductory music repeated)
Move into individual spaces. Repeat and develop some of the solo sequence in section 1 and determine own conclusion.

Resources used during the lessons include the video recording of *Waterless Method of Swimming Instruction* (1980) by Robert Cohan. The music, like the Pink Floyd piece suggested, should not have much beat or accent. It should be quiet and smooth like the music accompaniment for the video.

Lesson content leading to the finished performance of this dance can be found in the appendix, pages 195–201.

Ways in which the above dance outcome implements the programme of study for dance at key stage 3

(The words/phrases taken out of the programme of study are typeset in italic.)

• There are opportunities to teach students *methods of composition* because for each part of the dance, they are required to make phrases and link these phrases together. In order to make the dance feel a whole, students are also required to understand how to repeat and develop the phrase in section 1 for the conclusion. In addition, they need to learn how to make a transition between sections 2 and 3. This kind of work and the language used to set tasks develop the students' concepts of form in dance and their ability to employ principles of form in their compositions. They are also extending further their abilities to improvise, select and refine expressive movement content appropriate for the theme of the dance (KS1/2).

Students are given experience of a 'contact improvisation' *type of technique* in exploring content for section 2 of the dance. This may be new to them and therefore requires much sensitive preparation for partner work. In all this work students will be led to understand why the content has been selected and how it *communicates meanings* relating to the theme. In addition to the students' own work, reference to the professional dance work, *Waterless Method of Swimming Instruction*, will reinforce how a choreographer employs the *technique* of abstracting movement from a realistic context and elaborates it through use of *style*, rhythm and exaggeration for the purposes of *communicating meaning* in dance.

• In this dance outcome students are required to reflect the quiet and smooth qualities of the accompaniment in their compositions. Students should also be encouraged to *perform parts of and the whole dance* to their peers, and/or to an audience and *show sensitivity to the accompaniment* whilst they perform.

• There is little *set movement* in this dance outcome. However, the students are required to observe and copy at least one action phrase out of *Waterless Method of Swimming Instruction*.

• During the lessons there is opportunity for the teacher to give the students *written tasks*. They may be asked to write an account of the movements selected for section 1 and why they selected them. They may well record the group work content for section 3 and *describe* in detail the action chosen from the video and why it was selected. The teacher will need to create opportunities for *written and oral work* during the experiences leading up to the dance outcome.

• Work with the resource, *Waterless Method of Swimming Instruction*, could also lead to discussion of the style of the movements, costumes and set, especially in relation to the *context of time and place* for the theme of the work. The processes of description, analysis and inter-pretation of the students' own dance work and the work on video will be employed during the lessons culminating in *Pool Idling*.

All of the above presumes progression from key stage 1 through to key stage 3 and it would be expected that skills, knowledge and understanding acquired from years 1–8 would feed naturally into work for year 9.

Ways in which the above dance outcome implements the end of key stage statements for physical education in key stage 3

Statement a) The students will have *adapted principles of form (strategies)* in creating the dance phrases and transitions and in successfully link-ing the parts to make a whole. They will *devise strategies* of working with a partner to perform the 'contact' sequence in section 2 of the dance and strategies of working in a group for the 'instruction' part of the dance (section 3).

Statement b) The students will need to *adapt and refine their existing skills* in selecting and refining movements from their repertoire to answer the task for section 1 of the dance, for example. Similarly, they will base their new learning of partner work for section 2 and the group work in section 3 of the dance upon many previous experiences of working in twos and groups, including concepts such as leading, following, copying, complementing, contrasting and using different spatial relationships to give variety and interest to the work. In section 2 there is emphasis on *developing new* partner work *skills* which involve lifting, pulling away from, supporting, leaning on, sliding off, moving onto, round, through and off your partner. The *safety factor* is definitely paramount here and sensitive care for each other should be developed in this partner work.

Statements c) and d) The students will *practise and perform* parts and the whole of their dance *compositions*. Having first worked on the techniques required to perform the actions, especially new ones, they should concentrate on linking the actions, and colouring them with contrasting expressive qualities (continuous, slow and gentle in the introduction, and more energetic, strong and accented in section 2 of the dance, for example). Each section should be *practised to achieve coherence* with the music and continuity of expressive intention. Gradually the sections should be *performed* in succession ensuring that phrasing is clear and dancers are in the right place at the right time. Attention should be given to performance attributes, such as focus, alignment, posture, extension, projection and musicality in order to develop artistic dance performance skills. Memorising the movement content and *observing themselves* on video and *each other*, perhaps through use of check lists to *identify strengths and weaknesses* will help to *improve the quality of the performance*. The lesson plan outcomes on pages 200–1 in the appendix give a fuller account of what might be achieved through practice and performance of the movement composition devised by themselves.

Statement e) In section 2 of the dance, for example, students will gain some insight into the ways in which partners can work supporting each other physically and taking each other's weight in order to achieve the intended expressive outcome. The movement content here can be exhausting and needs to be performed co-operatively and sensitively to gain maximum effect. Close contact of partners, whether of single or mixed sex may at first be embarrassing for students of this age group, but experience of this kind of work can help to achieve healthy and natural attitudes about physical contact precisely because such contact has an expressive and artistic purpose. Again, reference to the video resource will help to focus the students' attention on the motivation of the dance rather than on everyday boy/girl relationships. These comments may be stretching the application of statement (e), but 'healthy' attitudes to the body in action with other bodies can, in my view, be achieved as well in dance activities as in especially designed health-related exercise programmes.

All of the above presumes progression from key stages 1 and 2 and the adaptation and refinement of existing skills, knowledge and understanding gained from previous dance experiences.

Ways in which the above dance outcome implements the theoretical basis of the midway *model*

The dance outcome *Pool Idling* clearly puts an emphasis on the fact that, in the art of dance model, dance lessons will always culminate in a dance or part of a dance. However, the means towards this end should definitely include all the elements of the *midway* model. So rather than the teacher creating and teaching the dance to the pupils (professional model) he/she will create a dance framework to ensure that they engage in the processes of creating, performing and viewing. Doing so will assist students' developing understanding, knowledge and skills with regard to choreography, performance and the appreciation of dances.

These creating, performing and viewing processes will be fully integrated although, at any one moment in a lesson, there will be emphasis on one more than another. The content of the lessons leading up to the dance *Pool Idling* in the appendix illustrates this (pages 195–200). Although in the list of lesson content there are clearly-defined composition tasks, performance tasks and viewing tasks, it is very likely that the teacher will require the students to engage in all three processes most of the time. For example, in the task to explore and identify content for section 1 of the dance, the students would no doubt be asked to watch each other and appreciate originality and appropriateness in the responses made. They might then work on improving the quality in their own (and perhaps each other's) performing of the movements. Although attention is focused on creating movements for this part of the dance, the processes of performing and viewing are employed to enhance the outcome.

In good practice, then, the integration of these elements will be apparent at many points in any one lesson. Moreover, at this secondary stage, there should be written and/or oral work where students describe, record, analyse, interpret and evaluate dances – their own, their peers' and professional dance works presented in live theatre or on video. Such work may well be supported by reading and research relating to a particular choreographer or dance work, all of which enhances appreciation and leads to further insight upon which students can base future choreographic and performance work.

1. Equal emphasis on process and product

As in the example discussed at primary level, the dance outcome/product, *Pool Idling*, is a qualitative whole having several related sections, a beginning, middle and end with repetitions, developments, contrasts, variety, climaxes, transitions and an overall unity in expressive purpose. It is important that the students in the secondary phase appreciate these formal and structural aspects of the dance outcome and that they start to perceive them in the dances they experience. However, the dance outcome itself is not the sole purpose of dance lessons. It *is* important, but not at the expense of worthwhile processes on the way. Teachers need to balance the achievement of a completed outcome with sufficiently deep and lengthy creating, performing and viewing processes. The time available needs to be carefully planned to ensure that sufficient attention is given to both process and product. The dance *Pool Idling* needs at least four hours of lesson time to complete. If less than this is available over three to four weeks, perhaps a shorter dance outcome is needed.

In developing an appreciation of the product, *Pool Idling*, students should also note that range and variety of expressive content are necessary attributes of a 'good' dance. However, their attention to the needs of the outcome (its expression of the theme, the overall variety and coherence of content) should not outweigh the attention given to the processes leading to the product. In attempting to achieve appropriateness, variety and originality of content an exploration task with equal emphasis on process and product might proceed in the following manner.

Extract from lesson plan

TASK – imagine you are indulging in the feeling of floating on the surface of a warm swimming pool. Explore and select arching, rolling, stretching, relaxing and curling movements. Start in a stretched lying position on your backs with arms above your head. Keep lying on and in contact with the floor most of the time but include one rising and falling action during your sequence. Keep the movements slow, fluid and continuous.

This is too long to give all at once so it might be split in the following way:

a) Exploration might start with improvisation of the floor movements to the music.

b) Demonstration of some interesting responses, the teacher's feedback and the suggestion of further images should broaden each student's range of movement ideas.

c) Concentration on linking the movements to make phrases and on variety should guide further the selection process.

d) Motifs could be viewed by peers and discussion take place to improve the selection and performance of the content.

e) Further exploration of the rising and falling actions could be interspersed with viewing some of these actions in the video of *Waterless Method of Swimming Instruction* and/or teacher-led exploration of lifting out of and falling into the floor.

f) The provision of a few ideas should encourage students to explore and find their own ways of performing these actions.

g) Create the sequence of motifs for section 1 of the dance (i.e. the task above).

h) Watch each other's work, comment and appraise. Practise to improve the quality of performance.

i) For homework, write down the content for this section of the dance and explain how the movements chosen convey the idea.

A range of processes could, therefore, take place to arrive at section 1 of the dance. These carefully planned and reasonably lengthy processes are more likely to achieve a rich outcome than taking shortcuts to complete the first section of the dance for the sake of having an end product. If, however, the lesson emphasises processes only and there is scant attention given to creating and performing something which can be repeated, there is little possibility of retaining the range and depth of the exploratory process for the following week.

Equal emphasis on process and product should be aimed at in the art of dance in education.

2. Equal emphasis on development of creativity, imagination and individuality and on acquisition of knowledge of theatre dance

The task given above for section 1 can be used to illustrate how a balance between developing the students' own creative responses and learning from the world of theatre dance can be maintained in the art of dance in education model.

The setting (an outdoor pool in sunny holiday weather), which is likely to be in the experience of the pupils, presents them with an imaginary canvas upon which they can place their own content. The starting position, the type of content and the fact that there should only be one incidence of rising and falling within the sequence is predetermined but this merely provides a framework or structure within which the students create their own movement ideas. The movements themselves are born out of each student's response to the task. As indicated in chapter 1 of this book, rather than dampen creativity, such limitations give the imagination a start and a secure base from which to travel freely. The range and originality of creative responses will depend on the quality of the exploration and teacher/student feedback, but opportunity is there in this and all other sections of the dance for individual, creative responses.

The form of section 1 of the dance with its starting position and one rise-and-fall action in contrast to the series of continuous, slow floor movements sets a good example of how to create form in a dance. This learning which, at this stage, should be made explicit to the students, feeds their growing understanding of form as it is presented in Western theatre dance works. The knowledge gained here about phrasing, contrast, climax and continuity should be re-inforced in creating section 2 of the dance where there is more freedom of choice in both the type and ordering of the content and this can usefully be reinforced by study of Cohan's work on the video.

The overall form in *Waterless Method of Swimming Instruction* – its sections and the transitions/contrasts of the dancer manipulating the deckchair, the abstraction of content from swimming itself, from Esther Williams-like swimming films and early twentieth-century approaches in swimming instruction – provides suitable exemplification of the process of abstraction and elaboration of movements to make dance motifs. Moreover, Cohan's constantly-changing use of the group in the space can be observed and discussed as an attribute providing variety and interest and the students should be encouraged to learn from this observation to enhance their own compositions. The duo sections can be used as starting points for exploration of content for section 2 of the dance and the moments of 'swimming' and land drill form the repertoire from which the students will select and copy a movement idea for section 3 of the dance.

This acquisition of knowledge of theatre dance through use of a video as stimulus and starting point for the students' own creative work provides what Best (1985) terms as 'grasp of the criteria of validity and value' in choreography. Hence pupils learn as much about the discipline through study of professional ready-mades as they do through responding to tasks within the bounds of their own imaginations. Indeed, it is often the case that students produce more creative and original responses when there are certain limitations than if given total freedom. In fact, the latter is more often than not counter-productive in that, unless experienced, students do not have an already built-in range of movement responses to tasks. Like words, movements need to be learned, stored, adapted and used appropriately before they can be said to be a part of the student's vocabulary. Given total freedom, without such a vocabulary, students of this age in particular will freeze and produce nothing.

On the other hand, there has to be a feeling of ownership of the product, too. It is important that there are sufficient creative opportunities included to allow for individual response so that most of the content in the dance seems to have been supplied by the students themselves. Even in the sections where direct reference is made to a resource, for example, section 3 of the dance *Pool Idling*, the students' own work should supersede the starting point and take on characteristics of its own. In fact this dance has an abundance of creative opportunity for the students. Their own ideas will develop in the partner and group work (sections 2 and 3) many of which will derive from their own experiences of playing in pools and of learning to swim.

Of course, the *midway* model for the art of dance in education supports a *midway* approach. The teacher's framework and professional resource create the limits within which the students' imaginations can have free rein. Creativity is nurtured and extended through carefully-structured learning experiences. The discipline and techniques of the art form have to be mastered, but it is not the chicken and egg situation commonly practised in the *professional* model. In the educational context, it is not necessary to master all the techniques first and serve apprenticeship for a long time prior to being able to create one's own dances. This might be perpetuated in professional dance learning circles but, in the art of dance in education, being creative and choreographing dances employing imagination go hand in hand with mastering of the discipline and learning from professional exemplars.

The methods employed to achieve these dual aims are discussed later. Perhaps at this stage, as in the case of the primary example discussed in chapter 2, if there is to be a leaning one way or the other, there should be rather more emphasis on the pupils' own creative work than on learning about theatre dance.

3. Equal emphasis on feelings and on training

It could be argued that the education of feelings/intuition discussed earlier in this book in the context of year 3 children, should be well advanced by the time year 9 is reached. If there has been a consistent dance education between these stages, pupils should have had many opportunities to express and experience feelings in response to dance situations. Each new idea with its implicit range of feelings will have required the pupils to explore and select appropriate movement vocabulary to express it. In this way, their repertoire of movement to communicate feelings will have enlarged and some understanding of associations between movements and feelings will have developed.

By year 9, it is probable that the students have learned that, in dance lessons, you do not express how you are feeling personally but learn how to communicate objective feelings through movements in formed dance compositions. Although the feelings are not real in the same sense as personal feelings, they nonetheless should be felt by the students through *getting inside* the dance idea. This is achieved through imagination – the feelings are imagined and communicated in dance. Hence, the importance of imagery and various stimuli such as music to accompany the dance, in order to inspire and extend the students' identification with feelings. Of course, it is only possible to imagine feelings that you have experienced in some way yourself. So the teacher needs to be sure that the pupils can bring sufficient understanding and knowledge of the feelings that they are attempting to convey in dance in order to be able to re-create them imaginatively.

The more experience of artistically-expressed feelings the choreographer, performer or viewer can bring to the dance situation in hand, the richer it will be. So it becomes a part of the dance teacher's task to provide as many feeling experiences as possible through the processes of creating, performing and viewing dances. In creating and performing dances, a range of ideas/themes, including abstract movement themes such as circularity, will offer the students opportunities to express many different feelings. In viewing dances (their peers' and professionally choreographed and performed dances), students will perhaps gain understanding of new feelings and ideas, thus extending further the boundaries of their imaginations. Study and appreciation of professional dance works are important means of expanding the students' experience and knowledge of life's feelings/meanings. So viewing dances also contributes much to an understanding of feelings and how dance can convey them.

The dance *Pool Idling* provides many opportunities for the students to imagine what it feels like floating in water, playing with a partner in water, learning to swim and so on. These imaginary situations linked to their own experiences conjure up a range of movement ideas to express the theme and the feelings it evokes. Each task outlined for the lesson content (see the appendix pages 195–200), provides opportunity for the students' own feelings and imaginings to enter into the expressive form. There is much opportunity, too, for the students to develop and utilise their growing sense of form in shaping motifs and phrases to create their dances. This knowledge is more often than not at an intuitive level in that they tend to make decisions about form because it 'feels right' rather than referring to guiding principles of form. By the end of key stage 3 students should have had many experiences of creating dances based upon the teacher's frameworks which, as indicated earlier, should have in-built coherence of expressive form. Through these experiences the students' subconscious knowledge is developed. When this is tapped, as Reid (1983) claimed, the pupils are said to be using intuition. They may not be able to say much about the form they have created but the decisions made through feeling what is right will indicate their understanding of form at the intuitive level. When the students have more experience, this understanding should become more conscious and objectively applicable to composing tasks.

Clearly then, both kinds of subjective feelings (those related to emotions and those related to intuitions) have important roles to play in the art of dance for secondary pupils. Yet, at the same time, students of this age are demanding more objective ends in that they desperately seek to develop sufficiently good technique in order to be able to perform the movements which capture the essence of those feelings. Secondary students in particular enjoy working the body to improve its facility and enjoy trying out new skills to add to their repertoire. After all, if they have danced from the age of five, they ought to be far beyond refinement of mere everyday movement to create their dance vocabulary. This may be the mainstay of the primary school child's vocabulary, but the secondary student needs to learn specific dance skills and practise dance movements which are far beyond the everyday roots. Hence, their running movements will include stylised extended runs, triple runs, turning waltz runs and the like, all of which emanate from one technique or another and contribute to the Western theatre dance forms' vocabulary of running. Such learning of specific dance vocabulary requires, to varying extents, a trained body in order that the vocabulary can be performed. The process of training to enable students to perform the movements required for a dance should develop hand in hand with new vocabulary. An example will help to clarify this.

In *Pool Idling*, section 1 requires the students to rise up and fall into the ground fluidly and slowly. Falling actions may not have been experienced very much before this dance so the teacher may elect to use this creative task as an impetus for acquisition of some skill and a further extended vocabulary of falling actions. The students' bodies must be properly warmed and prepared before they learn specific falls such as the Graham side fall, forward fall from a tip forward on one leg with the other extended high behind and reaching forward to land on parallel arms, forward fall initiated with slide towards side splits, backward fall rolling through the body to a back lying position and so on. These are just a few stylised and specialised falls the students may be able to add to their vocabulary. They need to learn how to perform them properly and will thus become more skilled in execution of them. Having acquired some skill in the context of specifically-learned techniques of falling, it is likely that the skills required for the students' own ways of falling will be of the same order. Once consolidated, knowledge and skill should be applicable to new and different falls developed as part of the students' creative responses.

A similar set of comments could be made about section 2 of the dance in that here the students need to learn some basic contact improvisation techniques. They need to be able to take each other's weight and to lift and put each other down safely and with control to achieve the expressive quality of the dance. Hence preparatory exercise and skill practices need to be built into the lessons before the students can create and perform the dance. This kind of training with clear objectives forms an important part of the students' experience in the art of dance. As well as learning the skills step by step and practising them, the students should be directed to view how the professional dancers perform similar movements in a study of Cohan's *Waterless Method of Swimming Instruction*. Here, analysis of where hands are put in order to lift, where the supporting person's feet are placed during the lift, where the accent is, how the lifted person keeps body tension, etc., will help the students to focus on technical points in order to help their own performance and on aspects of the skills in order to appraise each other.

Concentration on one or two technical requirements, such as those above within each dance outcome, will ensure that the teacher is giving sufficient attention to training the students' bodies whilst they acquire enough dance skills to fulfil the expressive needs of the dance. In this way, the objective ends of the *midway* model are playing a role although, perhaps at this stage, they should not be emphasised. Rather, for lower secondary students, if the balance is uneven, there should be rather more weight on the subjective feeling kind of education than there is on the objective training kind of education.

4. Equal emphasis on movement principles and on stylised techniques

It should be apparent to the reader that the content of the dance *Pool Idling* is derived from both the Laban-based movement principles and vocabulary based on two contemporary dance techniques – firstly, mainstream contemporary dance with a Graham flavour as exemplified by Cohan in particular – and, secondly, something like certain aspects of contact improvisation.

The principles of movement serve both the teacher and the students very well as means towards achieving the expressive outcome. Each section of the dance defines a kind or several different kinds of action to be created and performed. The word 'kind' here to preface actions is important because this explains exactly the role of the principles in forming a framework within which the students choose their own actions in preference to learning and employing a dictated set of steps.

Throughout the dance, there are examples of framework tasks which give scope for exploration and choice. The introduction defines only that the students travel slowly into different resting positions. The sort of steps they take, the combination of them, rhythm of them, direction they take and the ultimate position and how it is arrived at are each student's choice. Section 1 requires the students to explore and make motifs out of a range of actions – arching, curling, stretching, rocking and rolling – and to include one rising and falling action. This is very typical of a movement principle approach in that the kind of action is defined but its detail is left open so that an arching movement can be done with just the head, with the top of the spine, with the whole spine – lying on different parts of the body or sitting, kneeling, standing or even jumping. There are a number of ways in which the concept of arching can be interpreted. Each student has the freedom to explore different ways and to find different answers to the task than those of other students in the group. In addition, each student's use of the dynamic qualities will vary even though the group as a whole is moving slowly and with continuity.

Further differences will be seen in responses to tasks which are somewhat looser than the one above. For instance, section 2 of the dance provides a framework of different possibilities for interpreting the theme of playing in the pool with a partner. Here, students need to be led to explore several different movement principles to interpret the theme of the dance. Partner work concepts (such as assisted jumps, and lifting and lowering), spatial relationship concepts (such as through, under, over and round) and the time concept of slow motion are interpreted by the partners in their own ways to express the theme.

Movement principles are, therefore, important sources for the content of each dance outcome but they are not the sole source. As indicated already, in order that students extend beyond their natural everyday movement vocabularies, there is need for reference to specified dance techniques, each with its own range of stylised movement content. Through such references, knowledge of the art form of dance vocabulary as known in the public world is developed. Dance content is not restricted to that derived from each student in response to a task, it also emanates from the professional dance training and theatrical contexts.

A knowledge of some Graham-like falling actions has already been alluded to as a potentially valuable source of content for section 1 of the dance *Pool Idling*. The technique of falling needs to be carefully taught and if the falls are to capture the essence of the Graham style they need to be stylised with particular attention to its distinctive features. This particular style may be the most appropriate to try to capture in the dance as a whole since, in the exemplar, Cohan retains a distinctly Graham-based style in his work.

Even though dance vocabulary for section 2 may derive from a contact improvisation technique, the dance can be performed in the more extended and placed Graham-based style rather than in the more relaxed on-going fluid style associated with contact work. Adherence to one particular style in a dance is an important factor to consider if the dance is to achieve coherence. *Waterless Method of Swimming Instruction* provides an example of this even in the use of everyday movements which are stylised, rhythmically phrased and exaggerated to achieve a particular Graham look.

The Graham technique then can be a source of content not only in terms of movement vocabulary but in order to capture the essence of a style. Of course the specific technical vocabulary if properly performed defines the truly distinctive Graham style. However, because the technique is very complex and difficult to perform, the possibility of achieving a close resemblance to this style with year 9 pupils is very remote. A sense of the style can be captured and it is encumbent upon the teacher to know how to distil the essences which will colour the movements sufficiently to give the dance a Grahamesque look.

As already acknowledged, known techniques can be used as

sources of content for dance in secondary education. In the notes for the dance *Pool Idling*, there is reference to two known techniques for the purposes of extending the students' repertoires of movement. How the vocabulary is learned and made their own is the next topic to be discussed.

5. Equal emphasis on problem solving and on directed teaching

The dance *Pool Idling* is a teacher's framework composition with very little set movement content included. Indeed, the only set content is determined through the choice made by any group of four pupils for section 3 of the dance (they choose at least one swimming type of action to copy from the video of *Waterless Method of Swimming Instruction*; even this action is not directly taught by the teacher. In all the other work leading to composition of their dances, the pupils are led through creative problem-solving tasks. In my opinion, at this stage in education, the teacher needs to intervene in about eighty per cent of problem-solving occasions in order that the students responses to tasks progress and develop in range and variety. Otherwise students may become satiated by over-use of the same vocabulary of movement regardless of different themes.

The intervention that occurs, however, needs to be carefully handled so that the students do not feel a loss of ownership of their dance. In the exploration tasks leading to selection of content for the dance (see page 196 in the appendix), the students are given the frameworks – sometimes quite tightly restricted (1a and b) sometimes quite open (1c, d and e). The teacher then acts as a catalyst by making observations or, better still, providing the students with the means (mostly by questioning) of making observations about each other's work. The quality of the questions or teaching points on 'things to look for' determines the quality and depth of subsequent exploration. Sometimes creative learning can be greatly enhanced if the students all try out an idea, either the teacher's or (more often) one of the student's. This may involve a direct teaching approach so that the others absorb the movement by 'getting inside it'. During the processes leading to composition of the dance, however, there should be a strong emphasis on the problem-solving approach where the students are agents in their own learning.

Nevertheless, emphasis on a problem-solving approach does not mean that the directed teaching approach plays a minimal role. At the secondary stage, the students need to learn and practise movements and compositional devices which have been tried and tested and become a part of what constitutes dance in the public world. In performance oriented work, for example (see 3d on page 199 of the appendix), directed teaching is important in helping students towards efficient and correct use of the body. This task requires students to learn how best to lift each other while jumping and it would be damaging if students were not directed in appropriate distribution of the weight and positioning of the bodies in relationship. A directed teaching approach is also necessary in transmitting how to fall in section 1 of the dance and, if the teacher pays attention to the Graham style of falling, some aspects of this will be transmitted, too. It may be appropriate for the students to learn a style study – prechoreographed by the teacher in a Graham-based style – to help them stylise their own movements in their compositions.

At times, the students also need to be directed in what to observe in dance works – their own and professional ones – in order to learn facts about dance. This kind of learning (propositional knowledge) about dance is objective and testable and it is easy to use a directive/instructive teaching approach by setting students to read chapters and to fill in worksheets with answers to questions. Although this method reduces the time taken to transmit knowledge about dance, students who direct their own learning, even in this kind of work, in my view learn more of the facts in the end and are more successful in retaining them. A researching method might be appropriate and this can be labelled pupil-directed learning because the teacher provides the books, journals, pictures, music and video materials and some questions or a task, and the pupils search out the answers for themselves. Project books or work journals to be handed in for assessment can work very well in that pupils can record their own dance choreography and performance work, and the knowledge that they gain in viewing dances and researching for information about them.

6. Artistic education

The central purpose with the dance *Pool Idling* is to extend students' knowledge and understanding of what constitutes a dance and their artistic skills in creating and performing dances.

a) Understanding what a dance is:

By year 9 students should have understood what constitutes a dance in that they will have experienced many dances (mostly through the teacher's frameworks) which have formal and expressive features symbolising themes. They will be beginning to perceive principles of form such as variety, logical development and unity as means of achieving coherence in the dances they create and they will have learned ways in which movement in dance becomes symbolic. They should also know something about style and how this characterises dances and dance movement.

The students' learning about the nature of dances is enhanced by watching the professional dance work *Waterless Method of Swimming Instruction*. Concepts of form, expression and style become reinforced through such exemplars and these concepts inform the students' work.

b) Skills, knowledge and understanding gained through the processes of creating, performing and appreciating dances.

Creating

In creating the dance the students will experience a range of tasks – some more open than others – in order to determine the content. The teacher's dance framework will identify the kinds of movements to be included but the students need to explore and select within the categories in the framework. For example, for section 2 of the dance, students will be led to explore and discover a range of assisted jumps, movements onto and sliding off their partner, through, under, and round partner and lifting and lowering movements to give the impression of playing in water. Different partner-assisted movements within this task will be tried and decisions made as to which to keep and which to discard. The students will then need to make decisions on the order and juxtapositioning of the moves to make phrases which complement the music and appropriately express the theme. Linking of the movements with an emphasis on fluidity and smoothness to create the illusion of being in water and to achieve an interesting use of time and space gives plenty of opportunity for the teacher to promote artistic learning.

Temporal variations can be achieved through placing accents in different parts of phrases. A turning-assisted jump may involve a swing-like rhythm where the accent is in the middle of the movement. An alternative supported jump would place the accent at the end of the movement if the supporting partner were to catch and hold the elevation suspended landing. Variation in the length of phrases is also possible because the music has no distinct phrasing in this section. Rhythmic patterning of the partner movements should be an artistic consideration alongside learning how to use the music as accompaniment. The music selected for the dance is ideal for this section in that it is smooth and ongoing. Accents can be placed anywhere in the movement and phrases can extend over the length of musical phrases or several short dance phrases can be accommodated within one musical phrase. There should, of course, be some matching of accents, phrasing, tempo and rhythm between the music and the movements so that they are complementary.

Spatial interest can be achieved if students are encouraged to attend to the positioning and alignment of their bodies to the perceived 'front' of the dance so that the audience gains the best view. It will also occur if there is a variety of spatial relationship in the partner sequence, i.e. the sequence should include movements back to back, side by side, facing, one behind the other, movements round, over, on and off partner and several other variations. This variety helps to make the dance rich in visual patterning.

Repetition and development of content in the final part of the dance require students to employ the means of development they know – such as changing level, performing with different body parts, adding movements such as turns and travelling, changing the qualities and/or spatial patterning of the original movements. This repetition and development of movements used in the intro-duction and section 1 of the dance give the dance a unity and completeness in that the beginning parts are re-echoed at the end. Yet it is not exact repetition because the students are asked to develop some of the movements from section 1 in any order and then to determine their own conclusion. Use of such devices to give form to the whole reinforces understanding of the concept and a developing awareness of how to structure dances.

Learning how to abstract from everyday and swimming actions in order to create movements which symbolise the idea is an empha-sised aspect of artistic learning in this dance outcome. The students will be asked to imagine the movements as if they were actual and then to take the essence of them as bases to retain in their motifs and to elaborate them by adding, adapting and changing them into dance movements.

An example will help to identify the artistic learning that might occur here. If the students are asked to include a breast stroke and diving action in a sequence they will need to select which parts of the actions to retain. For example, they could choose the arm action in the breast stroke and the starting position with arms extended and together and a downward action for the dive. These can be made larger and changed to a degree but they should remain recognisable.

Further elaboration of the actions by the addition of travelling, jumping, turning or leg gestures and by the variety of qualitative and spatial aspects (except the downward emphasis in the dive) will make the original starting movements into developed stylised dance motifs which symbolise the idea.

Performing

In sections 1 and 2 the selected actions will need much practice to produce the appropriate slow-motion quality that will give the illusion of being in water. This demands control, balance, strength and co-ordination to link actions into fluid phrases. The phrases will, nevertheless, need to be accented in a way which complements the music and it should be clear where the highlights/climaxes occur.

In section 3 of the dance, the relationships with the other dancers in unison or canon will need to be practised and in section 2 the contact work will require much work to perfect the interactions which will convey the idea of being in water.

Technical proficiency in performing the movements should be developed with helpful comments from the teacher or peers to identify ways in which the movement might be improved. Gradually, with repetition, new skills will become embedded and old skills (e.g. jumps assisted by a partner) will be extended in different co-ordinations when performed in different contexts. The techniques of performing stylised jumping actions are discussed in further depth in the appendix page 199 and clearly such a progressive treatment of learning new skills will enhance the students' abilities to perform these and related movements well.

It is often beneficial at this stage in dance education to develop dance skills through a technical study approach. A technical study comprises dance skills demonstrated in motifs, phrases and sections to make a formed whole. It can last for about a minute but is usually about three minutes long. As in music, a study concentrates on a limited range of material in order that it is practised as fully as possible. A study, as its name suggests, requires study and challenges the dancer to work towards mastery of its content. A study should ensure that the learners are acquiring new skills to enlarge their vocabularies (which should include different dance styles) or to improve performance qualities.

In the context of *Pool Idling*, there are two sections which could benefit from preliminary learning of a dance study – falling and rising actions for section 1 or contact work in pairs for section 2. The teacher would need to decide which aspect to focus on and would need to create a dance study to another piece of music (if required at all) and teach it to the students in a directed way. The dance study should include a range of content but, more importantly, it should contain the differing technical processes necessary if falling or contact work is to be mastered. It should be used to introduce some ways in which the task in the dance might be answered but it should not exhaust the range of content appropriate to the task. Students should not feel constrained in their creative work by the technical study. Rather, it should act as a stimulating starting point for their own creativity. The main reasons for teaching a dance study – to improve technique and to introduce or develop vocabulary for the dance outcome – should be kept in mind. The dance study (as distinguished from a pure dance) should be treated as a means to the end and not an end in itself.

In terms of performance qualities, throughout the dance, students should endeavour to extend their movements, project to an audience, use focus appropriately and express their meanings. Practice of each of these features should greatly improve the performance overall.

Viewing

All of the above features in creating and performing the dance can be viewed by peers, on a video if a camera is available and by the teacher. Description, analysis, interpretation and evaluation of the elements in the dance can take place in order that students learn from others and improve their own work. It is also important to use the professional exemplar of *Waterless Method of Swimming Instruction* as a source of reinforcement of artistic learning. For example, the slow-motion, beautifully extended and controlled movements of the dancers diving from the edges into swim-like actions should provide much to discuss and learn from in order to improve the students' own performance qualities.

Appreciation

All of the learning in the context of creating, performing and viewing *Pool Idling* and *Waterless Method of Swimming Instruction* contributes to a developing appreciation of the constituent elements of a dance as an expressive, stylised and formed whole. Appreciation of the dance includes appreciation of each other's creative responses to the teacher's tasks and of the performance of the dance. Appreciation of *Waterless Method of Swimming Instruction* will also develop, especially if a resource-based teaching approach is used to guide detailed perceptions of its intrinsic qualities. This appreciation will inform and enhance the students' own work.

7. Aesthetic Education

In all the creating, performing and viewing experiences involved in producing the dance *Pool Idling*, the students should be encouraged to develop their aesthetic perceptions both as performers and appreciators.

In performing the dance, the students' awareness of the qualities contained in the movement – the slow, indulgent, luxuriating, stretches, arches and curls in section 1, for example – may be felt by the students' imagining themselves in a warm pool enjoying a feeling of well-being like that of a cat on a mat in front of a fire! This imaginary feeling would be triggered by the sensation of the movement itself in its slow, sensuous, indulging stretching and, in turn, the imaginary feeling should produce a more feeling and therefore qualitative movement outcome. The sensory and expressive qualities should be emphasised in the students' performances and the kinesthetic feeling of these will be aesthetically appreciated during their performances.

In viewing the dance or parts of the dance, the students should have many occasions to appreciate aesthetically the sensory and expressive qualities it contains. Looking at each other's work and guided by the teacher's questions perhaps, students can be encouraged to find words to describe the sensory qualities of, for example, buoyant, wave-like, swooping, entwining, wooshing upward movements in section 2 of the dance to express free playing in water with a partner – the floating, continuous and slow movements giving an impression of water round the pair. Use of analogy and metaphor feeds each student's imaginary perceptions of the dance and perhaps develops ability to perceive more in an aesthetic way.

The formal qualities of the dance and its parts should also be brought into focus in developing the students' aesthetic perceptions. Here attention given to the sections and how each develops logically into the whole provides a sense of unity which can be discussed as a pleasurable completeness when the dance has been viewed. (It may not produce this sensation, of course, especially if there are parts which do not seem to cohere. This, also, would be an aesthetic experience, a negative one). The repetition and development of motifs and of section 1 at the end of the dance, the linking transitions, the highlights and contrasts, the coherence of style, are formal qualities which contribute to the overall sensation of a meaningful whole dance.

Viewing of the professional exemplar should also help to develop the students' aesthetic perceptions. Here, they are free to interpret the meanings and feelings contained in the dance and should be given opportunities to express their perceptions in discussion and/or in writing. Again the use of descriptive words, analogy and metaphor, and sharing them in discussions may help individual students to open up alternative ways of viewing the work aesthetically. Attempts should be made to promote opportunities for the students to express what they feel about the work and whether they judge it to be good or not. Reasons for their feelings and judgements could be found through use of Osborne's aesthetic template in discussion of the perceived sensory, expressive and formal qualities.

Throughout the experiences leading to a final production of *Pool Idling* then, students' perceptions of their own work, their peers' work and of the professional exemplar could be enriched through application of an aesthetic approach to the processes of creating, performing and viewing.

8. Cultural education

Year 9 students will have absorbed many concepts underpinning mainstream choreography and performance in Western contemporary culture. These concepts include the ways in which ideas are translated into symbolic dance motifs, the use of the stage space and manner of presentation to an audience, the duration of time for a dance work and how the dance is put together to make a whole. Knowledge of expression and form is therefore developing and extending through each dance experience. Yet the kind of expression and form experienced in *Pool Idling*, with its reference to a contemporary dance piece choreographed by Robert Cohan, an American who was strongly influenced by Martha Graham, is very specific, i.e. it can be described as Western contemporary dance. There is much to be learned within this somewhat narrowly focused dance education since contemporary dance, like any other art form, has its own particular 'language' and artistic procedures. If students become conversant with terminology to describe the movements, become experienced in interpreting abstracted symbolic meanings and become able to discern form, they may well develop into informed audiences for contemporary dance (see also 2, page 87) and this is an important part of their cultural education.

Contemporary dance, however, is but one small part of a much larger domain. Dances with roles other than a theatrical role and derived from other genres need to be experienced in addition to those emanating from mainstream Western theatre contemporary dance contexts. This is necessary in order to broaden the students' concepts of the art of dance and dance generally – including folk and social dances, for example. (Some ideas for this kind of work are included in the appendix.)

In the dance discussed here and especially *Waterless Method of Swimming Instruction*, the theme and the way it has been expressed fall within an historical context. The early twentieth-century approach to swimming instruction and the references to 1930s' films provide one stylistic boundary, the Graham-based technique provides another. The students could be led to recognise these aspects as historical characteristics.

Their own dance pieces, however, will contain these elements only to a degree. The reference to the style and technique of contact improvisation, which was developed much later than the Graham technique (i.e. 1970s), will give the students' dance a newer look. A conscious attempt to make the students' own pieces reflect today's mainstream dance works rather than the professional exemplar could be advantageous in teaching the students something about style.

A dance artist's workshop and/or study of video material on the use of contact improvisation as a basis for choreography would help the students to discern the essential differences in style. Such learning helps to develop the students' understanding of the history of the art of dance.

RESOURCE-BASED TEACHING/LEARNING

The dance outcome and lessons leading to the final performance of it will have been enhanced and enriched by reference to professional dance exemplars, in particular, *Waterless Method of Swimming Instruction* and the dancers' performance of it. It is suggested above that this exemplar is used, for the most part, as a stimulus or as inspirational input in that it provides an extra resource that may indirectly assist the students' own creating and performing activities. In one section of the dance, the resource is used more directly in that the students are asked to copy one of the 'swimming' actions and to include it in their sequence. In these ways then, resource-based teaching can be seen to play a part in the dance experiences of the year 9 students.

Student-based learning is the distinguishing characteristic of resource-based teaching which at this level and beyond should, in my opinion, feature as an important part of the teaching process. The ideal situation of students working on their own with easy access to video recording and playback systems and to a library of dance resources may seem a little far fetched. Yet, in a situation where dance is centred in a studio or room with storerooms close at hand, it should not be a problem. In any event, even if the class has to be taught as one group, students can work from worksheets to find their own answers to tasks and then share these with the rest of the class. If there is just one video playback system, however, the teacher will either have to set group tasks with only one group at a time employing the system, or work through a worksheet with the class as a whole. The disadvantages of the latter are obvious.

Viewing tasks

There are three clear objectives for the use of Cohan's *Waterless Method of Swimming Instruction* as a resource to underwrite the dance experiences culminating in *Pool Idling*.

1. To identify and learn from the ways in which Cohan has abstracted from the starting points of being in water and learning to swim to develop dance motifs.

2. Through analysis of the video, to enhance learning about performance by reference to qualities in the dancing.

3. Through replication of one of the 'swimming' actions, to 'get inside' a part of the dance by performing it and thus experiencing how Cohan abstracts and develops the action, gives it rhythm, style, expression and form.

The teacher could employ a resource-based teaching methodology for each of these objectives, and viewing tasks would feature as necessary starting points within a teaching/learning programme.

For example, in identifying the process of abstraction, students could be asked to watch the sequence from the point where the women are hanging from the side of the pool and the men lift them off into performance of two duos, up to these duos performing two lifted jumps where the women touch their toes. Students could be asked to:

a) identify three swimming-type actions and describe what is added and/or taken away from the actions to make them into dance movements;

b) identify other movements which indicate that the dancers are in water;

c) identify recognisable dance movements and name them if possible (e.g. *arabesque* from ballet and contraction and release from contemporary dance);

d) notice the way that the two duos relate in space and in use of unison and canon.

Further viewing tasks should include viewing of the whole work and questions to develop the students' aesthetic perceptions of it. Viewing tasks will also necessarily precede creating and performing tasks which derive from the resource.

Creating tasks

Several of the creating tasks could be supported by use of the resource and a resource-based methodology. A creating task could follow the viewing of *Waterless Method of Swimming Instruction* and might proceed as follows:

• in pairs, with one dancer using the arm actions of a back stroke, find ways of leaning away from your partner (as on the video when using breast stroke in the above described section of the resource) and develop the movement into a phrase including travelling, turning and jumping.

A further task leading to section 3 of the dance might take the following form:

• using the beginning duo and subsequent quartet in the resource, select a swimming type of action to copy;
• noting the changes of relationship within the duo and quartet;
• noting the use of unison and canon in this section of the dance;
• in fours, creating the sequence for section 3 of the dance employing the copied movement from the video and, if you wish, some ideas for orchestration of your motifs.

This task starts using the video in a direct way – copying a movement – and then indirectly as a stimulus or starting point for revision of ways in which relationships can be varied and motifs can be orchestrated in a four.

In such ways, the resource can be used to reinforce artistic learning that has already been undertaken in creating dances and to introduce new learning. The resource should be used more as an impulse for the students' own creative work rather than something to be replicated. Carefully designed tasks will help students towards this kind of resource-based learning whilst creating their own dances.

Performing tasks

There are many ways in which the performance on video can be used as a teaching/learning tool. The dancers on it demonstrate very well the slow motion quality to give the illusion of being in water and their extension, control, balance, line, projection, continuity and fluidity in use of their bodies is exemplary. Students may be given tasks to identify some of these qualities and develop knowledge that will improve their own performances. For example, in watching the two men dance their opening duo, they could proceed as follows:

a) watch carefully how the dancers use their knees and feet to convey buoyancy in water while jumping;

b) take note of what the arms are doing to help;

c) also note the degree of tension in the body to help produce the upward lift in the movements even when landing;

d) work in twos, one observing and one performing, to help each other achieve the same buoyancy.

Another task may be focused on continuity and fluidity and here the performance of the three women in the section following the above duo makes a fine example. The students could practise for themselves:

a) the hands together snake-like action of arms into the side roll and rise, concentrating on smooth, continuous and fluid action with no jerks or stops;

b) the undulating arms and upper body actions;

c) moving through a) to b) and repeat keeping the qualities as fluid as in a);

d) now dance your own partner sequences using the same qualities, having discussed where it is appropriate to do so.

Using the video in this way to improve performance brings great benefit in that, once students can see performance attributes as they are pointed out, they know what requires attention in their own work. It is much easier to work from an intellectual understanding of what is to be strived for than to take instruction from the teacher to improve performance. Seeing it in action and conceptualising what it is that makes it good performance abolishes the need for many words and many trial and error practices. The latter without an image can be slow and unproductive. Using a video such as this, with tasks carefully structured to ensure observation of the range of qualities contained in the dancers' performance of each and every movement, can be extremely valuable in promoting an aesthetic response in students which can then be used as inspiration to feed their own endeavours.

Cultural/historical tasks

The kind of knowledge and understanding which can be gained from study of *Waterless Method of Swimming Instruction* as a cultural/historical phenomenon has already been discussed in 8 (page 102). Use of a resource-based teaching/learning methodology, however, will ensure that students develop this knowledge and understanding for themselves.

For example, to study the Grahamesque style of the dance, students could be asked to study a prepared handout which lists principles and characteristics in the Graham technique and then to find incidences of these in a selected section of the work.

Another task requiring written responses might aim to develop the students' understanding of the time and place setting of the theme. Pictures of early twentieth-century cruise ships, costumes, and writings on methods of teaching swimming through land drill exercises, together with programme notes, critics' writings and any other such materials could be used as reference resources in order to complete exercises such as the following:

a) Study this picture (either held on pause or scanned off the video opening tableau if not available from other sources), identify the time and place it indicates and list the features in the picture which helped you to make this decision.

b) Describe the costumes in *Waterless Method of Swimming Instruction* and comment on their authenticity in the context of the time and place setting of the dance.

c) Write a short description of how the choreographer used land drill exercises in the dance and on how other swimming aids indicate the time and place of the dance.

Such work might best be done when introducing the resource to the students rather than at a time when they are getting to know it well. To develop further their understanding of the context of the piece, additional tasks might include viewing snippets of 1930s' to 50s' films of synchronised swimming in order to identify the possible derivation of Cohan's dance ideas.

Resource-based teaching/learning pays dividends in developing the students knowledge, understanding and skills in viewing, creating and performing dance/s. It can also develop a deeper aesthetic appreciation of a dance work which, in turn, promotes an improved ability to aesthetically perceive other dance/s.

Conclusion

This chapter, on the art of dance in secondary schools, illustrates how understanding and application of the theoretical basis for the art of dance in education (presented in chapter 1) can lead to effective delivery of the National Curriculum programme of study and end of key stage requirements for key stage 3.

As in the chapter on primary dance education, the aim here was to demonstrate in detail how the theoretical basis underpins practice and, again, only one example dance outcome and some of the teaching/learning that led up to its completion, was scrutinised to illustrate this theory. This detailed application of theory to practice should help teachers understand what, in my view, constitutes good practice in teaching the art of dance in secondary education. Having applied the theoretical basis for the art of dance to this one practical situation focused on year 9 students, teachers should be able to apply it to different year groups.

At the time of writing this book, teachers of dance in secondary education are very short of texts to help them in planning progressive dance content (schemes and units of work and lesson plans), for key stages 3 and 4 and for dance examinations such as GCSE, AS and A level. To this end, the appendix provides an interpretation of the programmes of study for key stages 3 and 4 (which of course includes much of the work appropriate for the GCSE level examination) and the text below provides some guidance as to how the theoretical basis discussed in chapter 1 can be employed to inform and improve practice in teaching GCSE, AS and A level dance courses.

THE ART OF DANCE IN EDUCATION AT GCSE, AS AND A LEVEL

To show how the theoretical basis for the art of dance in education is also applicable to the above examination syllabuses, it is perhaps necessary, first to outline and describe the contents of the syllabuses.

GCSE – Northern Examining Association Syllabus for 1994

(Passages in italics below are directly quoted from this syllabus).

This syllabus defines clear assessable objectives and content for the examination course. It states that *candidates will be required to show knowledge and understanding of the terminology, concepts and principles covered by the subject content in the three areas of performance composition and appreciation.* It also states that *interrelationships between the three general headings are important and must be emphasised throughout the course.*

The objectives are listed as follows:

PERFORMANCE
Candidates will
1. *show knowledge and understanding of performance;*
2. *show in dance performance the level of technical competence and expression that has been achieved.*

COMPOSITION
Candidates will
3. *show knowledge and understanding of composition;*
4. *compose dance which successfully communicates the artistic intention of the choreographer.*

APPRECIATION
Candidates will
5. *show knowledge and understanding of context;*
6. *describe, interpret and evaluate dance showing accuracy, imagination and sensitivity.*

The scheme of examination includes the following:

Performance – in a dance either from known repertoire or choreographed by the candidates, teachers or peers;
– of a set study at the end of the course.

Composition – a solo or a duo or a group dance presented at the end
of the course.

Assignment – a course work project which can include practical
work. As stated in the syllabus: *ten study areas have been identified in
the syllabus and sixteen tasks devised to be compatible with the study
areas.* Candidates are required to focus on a single study area and
select two tasks from the list. The study areas include study of a
dance work, a choreographer, a company, a dance artist, a dance
era, a dance style, dance notation, dance in the local community, the
relationship of dance to music or design.

Written paper – a single one and a half hour unseen paper. The
sample paper accompanying the 1994 syllabus requires that students
view a video extract of *Waterless Method of Swimming Instruction.* The
questions are less focused than those suggested above for year 9
students. For example, with reference to the snippet employed
above where the three female dancers enter the swimming pool, the
students are asked:
. . . . *what do their movements suggest?* and they then have to give two
reasons for their answer. This is a more open-ended task and
requires the students to show their knowledge of sensory and
expressive qualities in the movements and their understanding of
how the actions, qualities, rhythm and spatial elements contribute
to the expression.

Advanced and Advanced Supplementary – Dance – University of London School Examinations Board

There are two options in both the above examinations. This ensures
that candidates who wish to study dance without performing in the
examination themselves may do so.

(Passages in italics below are directly quoted from the syllabuses).

A LEVEL	AS LEVEL
OPTION A	OPTION A
Paper 1 (practical) 40%	Paper (practical) 60%
Choreography of a duo or group dance	Choreography of a duo or group dance
Choreography and performance of a solo	Choreography and performance of a solo
Performance from a notated score	OR
Performance of a prescribed solo	Performance of a prescribed solo.
Paper 2 (written) Section A – short answer questions	Paper 2 (written) Section A – short answer questions
Paper 3 (written) Questions on set works Questions on broader issues	
OPTION B	OPTION B
Paper 1: (practical) 26%	
Choreography of a duo or group	
Choreography of a solo (candidates do not normally perform either of the above)	
Performance of a notated score	
Paper 2 (written) Section A and B (the latter is a prepared topic)	Paper 2 (written) Section A and B (essay)
Paper 3 (written) Section A (set works) and B on broader issues	Paper 3 (written) Knowledge of TWO dance works in TWO genres

The *above* practical work in both examinations can be in a selected genre from African (*all the dance styles of Black culture in sub-Saharan Africa and Caribbean culture*), Ballet (*Western classical ballet styles evident in present-day repertoire*), Contemporary Dance (*styles which have emerged in Western Europe and North America in the twentieth century and have been called variously free dance, barefoot dance, natural dance, modern dance, contemporary dance, post-modern dance, new dance, etc.*), or Indian Dance (*focus on one or more of the major classical styles of the Indian sub-continent – Bharata Natyam, Kathak, Kathakali, Manipuri, Mohiniyatam, Odissi. The study may be in the classical tradition or in the Tagore or other contemporary styles. It may be supported by experience of Indian folk dance styles.*)

The set works for both syllabuses include an African dance (e.g. *Coming Home* (1988), Dzikunu), a ballet (e.g. *Les Sylphides* (1909), Fokine), contemporary dance works (e.g. *Sergeant Early's Dream* (1984), Bruce; *Soda Lake* (1981), Alston) and an Indian dance (e.g. *The Return of Spring* (1987), Dananjayan). Those mentioned here were set for the 1993 examination.

The content requires that all students study choreography in order that they can choreograph themselves and/or in order that they can analyse and discuss in depth professional choreographers' works. This will include study of the theme of the dance work, treatment of the theme, and presumably style of the dance work/s. Surprisingly, unless it is subsumed under the heading of *character of the dance*, style is a missing feature in the published list of content. To this end, constituent features of movement – actions, dynamics, spatial and relationship features are studied alongside physical (performance environments) and aural settings (music/sound). Form in dances is studied through analysis of compositional devices (motif/phrase, development, variation, repetition, contrast, climax, balance, proportion, logical sequence and unity) and structuring of the dance works into sections (binary, ternary, theme and variation, rondo, episodic). These features of form are studied in relation to the music/sound.

All students are also required to study performance though those who opt for option B in both examinations do not have to perform themselves. However, in order to be able to choreograph effectively and to be able to write about performance, it is important to develop the students' understanding of its constituent features (particularly, it is assumed, those pertaining to style).

Appreciation plays a major role in both syllabuses. Here, theory of choreography and performance is enhanced and extended through a study of the historical and cultural contexts of the genres and dance works studied. Students are required to show knowledge and understanding of the function of dances as determined by *changing performance milieu, and relationship to other dances in the same genre and to other art forms.*

Applying the theoretical basis to GCSE, A and AS level examination syllabuses

Clearly, the theory in chapter 1 and the range of content and methods which, in this section, exemplifies the theory with reference to year 9 students, are all relevant to the teaching of the art of dance at GCSE level. Moreover, although the AS and A level syllabuses appear on the surface to introduce different dance forms, i.e. African, Classical Ballet and Indian, a brief reading of them will show that the conceptual basis underlying the work and the content examined is still that pertaining to the art of dance.

The three processes – creating, performing and appreciating – are central to these syllabuses, though the emphasis is perhaps even more towards the products/outcomes (i.e. choreography, performance and appreciation) of the art of dance than for secondary students in year 9 or below. Nonetheless, the processes involved should be experienced fully too because, as made clear throughout this book, a qualitative process leads, more often than not, to a qualitative product.

In examining a GCSE dance composition, for example, the following criteria of assessment will be applied in the 1994 examination:

a) *degree to which the dance provides an ***appropriate*** response to the ***original*** idea or stimulus.*

b) *content*
   i) *rhythmic, dynamic and spatial interest.*
   ii) ***originality*** *and* ***imaginative*** *use of movement.*

c) *structure*
   i) *repetition and climax*
   ii) *logicality of progression of phrasing in relation to the theme*
   iii) *development of initial material*
   iv) *variety and contrast in relating to thematic material*
   v) *unity of the whole work.*
(* author's emphasis)

Out of 30 marks there is a scale of grading descriptors. The bottom defines a bare minimum (not very clearly), i.e. *a response which merely continues and uses a limited vocabulary.* The top defines the expected outcome as:

> An articulate and highly refined response to the original idea; it will, in addition, show a sophisticated use of rhythms, dynamic and spatial combinations. There is evidence of an

extremely effective use of contrast, climax and logical sequence, the whole shows considerable understanding of compositional form. The result is an exceptionally well realised and unified dance.

Top marks are awarded for performance if the candidates *successfully combine technically accurate movements and excellence in body control with sensitive interpretation of the expressive qualities*. Furthermore, in the context of the assignment, top marks are awarded if the candidates show:

> Detailed knowledge and a high level of understanding of the study areas. The tasks have been completed with accuracy, imagination and sensitivity resulting in an exciting and original assignment.

These descriptions indicate a level of achievement, knowledge and understanding which, in my view, would be difficult to attain without attention given to *both*

• process *and* product;
• creativity, imagination, individuality (note words in the author's bold in the criteria of assessment of composition) *and* acquisition of knowledge of theatre dance;
• feelings/subjectivity of experience *and* training for performance;
• understanding of generally applicable movement principles *and* specific dance styles as sources of content;
• the full range between problem-solving *and* directed approaches in teaching dance.

This points to the fact that, for the above examination syllabuses, teachers should be delivering a *midway* model incorporating a balance of features derived from both the *educational* and *professional* models. The work involved clearly constitutes an artistic education in that the syllabus content lists the skills, knowledge and understanding of the art of dance which students are required to study through the processes of creating, performing and appreciating dances. It is also clear that study of the historical and cultural aspects of the art of dance, particularly in the A and AS level, gives the students contexts in which to place their dance experiences.

The broader cultural contexts of the A and AS level syllabuses are a welcome development in the study of dance in education. However, as stated above, this is not departing from the consensus art of dance model. Rather, it is expanding on the styles of dance which can be included in the model. The African and Indian dance styles are those used in presentation dances (i.e. the performing art form) emanating from these continents. The list of content in both syllabuses requires that these genres alongside contemporary dance and ballet, be studied as art forms.

The three strands of choreography, performance and appreciation are the organising art of dance concepts in which all the dance experiences within the courses are framed. Hence the *midway* model of the art of dance in education is merely expanded through access to different styles of dance in these syllabuses. It is not replaced by any other model.

Whether or not the study of dance at GCSE, A or AS level contributes to the students' aesthetic education is entirely in the hands of the teacher. The criteria of assessment of choreography and performance imply that feeling, imaginative and sensitive presentations will be rewarded high marks, but there is no mention of the word 'aesthetic' anywhere in the syllabuses. Perhaps this is due to the fact that aesthetic perception and feelings are hard to identify and impossible to assess. Yet, how do examiners rate levels of sensitivity? What constitutes imagination, originality and sensitivity at GCSE level as opposed to A level? These and many more questions need answers if it is claimed that dance can contribute to aesthetic education.

Perhaps most teachers would say that aesthetic education is delivered through the appreciation sections of the syllabuses and, certainly, there is an element of truth in this premise. Questions such as *What is the mood of this extract? Explain how the following help to create this mood – movement qualities, accompaniment, lighting.* (GCSE Sample Paper 1994) demand that the candidates interpret the mood which emanates from the dance piece and imagine the feelings/meanings associated with the movement qualities, accompaniment and lighting. This requires an aesthetic and subjective feeling response and it also requires that students have learned to respond in this way with the appropriate language. The range of answers provided in the sample is limited, but there is some evidence of acceptance of negative as well as positive aesthetic responses and differences of interpretation.

A perusal of the above GCSE papers and the 1993 A and AS level papers shows little evidence to support the case that aesthetic education is a necessary part of these courses. However, if teachers set tasks which aim to develop students' perceptions of aesthetic qualities, their answers to such questions as the above and to Section B of Paper 3 in A level (1993) for example, will be deep, rich, imaginative and individual. The latter reference to A level requires a comparison of two reviews and the students are asked to *consider the extent to which each critic illuminates the constituent features of the dance, the form of the dance, the significance of the dance and the performance of the dancers.* There is much in these reviews that could be labelled aesthetic language; many metaphors are used and reference to sensory, expressive and formal qualities permeate the writings. This suggests that teachers who employ such a framework to direct their students' perceptions may enable their students to do better in such questions than students who do not have such opportunities.

As made clear throughout this book so far, resource-based teaching would seem to be an ideal way of delivering the art of dance in education so that all the facets of the *midway* model, including its contribution to aesthetic education, are covered simultaneously.

Use of the set dance works (and others with which to compare them) as bases for resource-based teaching of the syllabuses, provides the teacher with a means of reinforcing and extending the students' knowledge and understanding of choreography and performance because the students can analyse and learn from the professional exemplars. The use of worksheets to help direct the students' perception of the qualities in the choreography and performance has already been identified as a non-directive way of developing the students' own abilities in choreography and performance. Moreover, if an aesthetic template were to underpin questions on worksheets, students would develop their ability to appreciate the works aesthetically. This sort of study promotes opportunities for the students to 'get inside' the professional dance works, which surely must improve their ability to write about them in the examination.

In the context of GCSE, A and AS level courses, resource-based teaching/learning is, in my view, an essential methodology to employ in successfully combining the study of professional dance works with study of choreography and performance per se. Resource-based teaching/learning is also a means of implementing the theoretical basis of the art of dance in education expounded in chapter 1 of this book.

It is further contended that comprehensive consideration of all the facets of the theoretical basis for the art of dance in education would enhance and enrich the teaching of dance at GCSE, A and AS level.

4

The Art of Dance in Higher Education

Background – and differences in approach

Dance in higher education, alongside other arts subjects, has been continually challenged to support its claim for academic status. As a subject always under threat, dance has surprisingly achieved much over the past decade or so to establish itself as a worthwhile area of study. However, it has not been able to avoid becoming a victim of recent economic cuts in higher education. There are not as many dance courses as there were in the 1970s/80s, but the range and level of content within them is much improved.

It is not intended here to discuss the historical development of dance in higher education in detail. For the purposes here, this history is only of interest in so far as shifts between what has been labelled in chapter 1 as the *educational* and *professional* models can be discerned. The main concern of this section, is to study the effects of these shifts of emphasis upon today's practice and to learn how the theory underpinning the *midway* model for the art of dance in education also applies in the higher education context.

Balance between theory and practical elements

There have been different emphases and balances between theory and practical elements of the courses. In the 1970s/early 80s, in Britain, the swing towards academic study of dance (mostly through relating it to other disciplines, e.g. psychology, sociology, aesthetics, anthropology) became emphasised because of the perceived need to be more accountable and creditable in an academic environment in which all students took degrees rather than certificates. However, the balance has been redressed and, in my experience at present, there seems to have been a shift from theory towards more practical work

117

in first degree courses. This may be due to the fact that validating bodies, most prominently the Council for National Academic Awards, became supportive in valuing practical activity as equivalent to theory. As a result, content, methods and assessment procedures within degree programmes have been developed which can be considered equally as rigorous as those of science-based courses. This is the premise. In practice, dance lecturers still have to 'fight their corner' for equality.

The nature of dance courses in higher education
In 1965, when I first started lecturing in a college for specialist physical education teachers, dance was taught in the form of the variously-called Modern Educational Dance/creative dance/movement education, established by Laban. It had become part of most teacher training courses for primary and for physical education teachers in the period from 1944 until the early 1970s.

Dance specialist teachers were trained at the Laban-based Art of Movement Studio from 1946 until it moved to London to become the Laban Centre for Movement and Dance in 1976. Dance specialist teachers were also trained at Dartford for a one-year Certificate of Education course for those who had completed a three-year course at the London College of Dance and Drama (a private dance teacher training college which had been established in 1944). Both these courses, and there were others in specialist and general colleges of education, focused almost exclusively on Laban's Modern Educational Dance approach which was considered the most suitable for teaching in schools.

In this *educational* model context, students found themselves exploring Laban's movement principles and creating responses to stimuli in the same ways in which they, in their forthcoming teaching roles (a dominant vocational outcome), would expect their pupils to explore and respond. They sometimes created dances of their own but, more often than not, these were freely improvised responses to sequences of tasks and there was no concern for compositional structure or principles of form. There was no reference to the *professional* model or to choreographers' works; there were few dance artists who visited educational establishments and those that did were ballet artists; there was no knowledge of contemporary dance techniques or methods of teaching dance composition.

Indeed, it was not until the summer of 1965 that a course in American modern dance was offered for lecturers at Dartington

College of Arts. This course (the first of many yearly courses) and the subsequent opening of the London Contemporary Dance School 1966 injected new approaches into dance courses in higher education.

The American modern dance model, with its emphasis on technique and the teaching of compositional skills (Graham, Humphrey and Cunningham approaches) caused a swing towards the *professional* model in higher education in the 1970s and 1980s. The extreme of this approach can be likened to the training of dancers in classical ballet at the Royal Ballet School and other such conservatoires. The London Contemporary Dance School has continued along the same lines as a training ground for professional dancers and choreographers. Although it has diversified to include a degree course and provides courses for teachers/lecturers and children, the content it delivers is essentially based on the *professional* training oriented model. Ironically, the Laban Centre for Movement and Dance also adopted the American modern dance model when it moved to London and it, too, has developed into a high-level training establishment for dancers and choreographers. Although a study of Laban's work has remained on the curriculum, it is dominated by content best described as a *professional* conservatoire curriculum.

Currently in Britain, students who wish to study dance of this kind in order to become professionals have to compete for a place in such privately funded higher education institutions. (They can apply for a discretionary grant but at the time of writing, this has become a very rare award.) The conservatoire approach in which the *professional* model has been developed and improved, does not constitute what could be called the mainstream art of dance in higher education model. This remains the province of some of the old colleges of education many of which later became polytechnics and now universities.

Today, dance is taught in some of these higher education institutions in the context of bachelor of arts single, double or combined honours degrees and, increasingly, in master's degree courses and above. In most bachelor degree courses, students select modules in dance such as technique and performance, choreography, repertoire, notation, history, aesthetic theory and cultural studies related to dance and sociology of dance.

The kind of practical dance most frequently found in such institutions can loosely be labelled contemporary dance in that it derives from American modern dance techniques (in America it is called modern dance) created between 1930 and 1960 by Humphrey,

Graham, Cunningham, Limon and Hawkins, and those of early European (mostly German) modern dance choreographers such as Jooss, Wigman and Holm. (These are the most influential early American and European modern dance exponents – there are others.) Today, these more traditional contemporary dance forms are frequently mixed with current contemporary, post-modern or new dance forms created by choreographers/dance makers such as Brown, Tharp, Gordon, Rainer, Paxton, Monk and Morris (Americans), Bausch, De Keersmaeker, Marin, Vandekeybus (Europeans) and DV8, Booth, Clark, Spink, Davies, Butcher and several others in Britain.

The list of renowned choreographers above, whose work constitutes an important part of the basis of study for degree students, points to the fact that in higher education, there has been a swing from what is labelled the *educational* model to the *professional* model. However, outside the conservatoires, this swing, though fairly extreme in the 1970s and early 1980s, has somewhat settled towards what I have labelled a *midway* approach to the art of dance in higher education.

The art of dance in higher education – an example

In order that dance in higher education can be analysed and to determine the validity of my claim that the approach most commonly practised is that which has been described in this book as a *midway* approach, the dance modules offered in a combined BA Hons. modular degree course in one institution are outlined below. It is considered that since these modules form part of a relatively new modular degree (1990 – present), they provide suitable examples of current practice. This judgment is not made in isolation. Since the author has been involved as an external examiner and validator of courses in many of the institutions that offer dance courses for similar degrees, there has been ample opportunity to compare them and discern common practices.

Undergraduate dance study in the institution chosen as an example is organised within a programme in which students can opt to specialise in dance, in drama, or they can take a mixture of the two. Some modules combine both dance and drama and the core theoretical modules underpin all dance and drama modules within the programme. Students also select modules in one or two other programmes to design their own modular degree course.

This brief outline of the place of dance within a modular degree alerts the reader to the fact that dance study in many British universities constitutes a part of a whole. It is not a conservatoire form of training. Rather, it aims towards developing knowledge, understanding and skills in dance which can be applied to a range of vocational outlets, such as animateurs, community dance workers, dance company administrators, arts management, dance publicity or education officers, dance critics, archivists, dance teachers and the like. Students select their modules according to interests, strengths and perceived vocational intentions.

Dance modules on offer at present are as follows:

• Dance Technique and Performance modules . . . . in all 3 years
• Choreography modules. . . . . in all 3 years
• Reconstruction Workshop modules . . . . in all 3 years
• Naturalism and Expressionism in Dance . . . . in year 1
• Dance on Film and Television . . . . in year 3
• Dance and Politics . . . . in year 3

Modules which combine study of dance and drama are as follows:

• Period Study . . . . in all 3 years
• Theatre Techniques . . . . in year 2

Compulsory core theory modules which underpin both dance and drama:

• Aesthetics and Culture . . . . in year 1
• Theoretical Approaches . . . . in year 2

Further details of the dance content in the above modules provide necessary information for the purposes of this section.

• *Dance technique and performance modules in year 1* take the form of study of the technique devised by Martha Graham. This has been selected as the initial foundation upon which understanding of today's contemporary dance can be built. Students participate in rigorous technical classes to acquire dance skills and Graham-based contemporary vocabulary. The class content – floorwork, centre practice and travelling – culminates in sequences and style studies through which students become acquainted with the style and become able to perform longer pieces in a Graham-based technique. Performance skills, such as alignment, focus, projection, rhythm, musicality and expression are practised and improved. The underlying principles and theories of the technique are studied through reading and writing assignments. Assessments take the form of classwork, short style studies, longer dances choreographed to include a range of Graham-based technique and opportunities for the students to demonstrate their performance skills and written work.

• *Dance technique and performance modules in year 2* extend the students' abilities and range of vocabulary through study of another contemporary technique such as that devised by Limon, Humphrey or Cunningham. Again, an understanding of the style and content is developed through practical classwork, style studies and longer dances, and principles and concepts underlying the selected technique are studied through research, reading and writing assignments. Assessments are more complex and expectations higher. Students' physical skills should be vastly improved at the end of year 2 and their contemporary dance vocabulary in these more traditional forms should be well established as a secure base from which to experiment in newer techniques in year 3.

• *Dance technique and performance modules in year 3* introduce different techniques which have emerged as a result of recent/post-modern choreography. For example, release techniques, contact improvisation, street dance, jazz and African dance techniques provide varied and different vocabularies of movement which may be more suited to present-day choreography.

• *Choreography modules in year 1* engage students in the basic processes involved in choreography (exploration, improvisation, selection and refinement of movement content to create symbolic expression) and require students to demonstrate an understanding of traditional principles of form in choreographing dances. Students are set tasks and learn from each other in sharing the outcomes. They also learn from analysis of professional choreographers' works.

• *Choreography modules in year 2* continue to develop students' abilities to choreograph in a conventional way. There is more emphasis on creating for groups and much is learned through examination of professional dance works choreographed by established modern dance mainstream practitioners. The module includes choreographic tasks, analysis of videos, presentation of seminars, reading and writing. Assessment is usually focused entirely on the choreography of group dances.

• *Choreography modules in year 3* include study of various post-modernist approaches. This work opens and broadens the students' concepts of choreography, its themes, content, form, style, environment and purpose. In order to do this, students explore the works and processes of artists such as Paxton, Rainer, Brown, Gordon, Childs, Tharp, De Keersmaeker, Vandekeybus, Bausch, Booth, Spink, Butcher and Anderson. They are assessed through presentation of a workshop based upon research into the work of one these post-modern/new dance artists and upon their own choreography. Their final piece of choreography may combine mainstream and post-modern practices or take either approach in a more purist way. It is required to be a substantial piece of work reflecting elements of current practice in professional choreography.

• *Reconstruction Workshop modules in all three years* aim to develop the students' knowledge and understanding of professional dance works through learning and performing excerpts from four works. Year 1 students learn parts of traditional works such as Fokine's *Petrushka* (1911) and Nijinsky's *L'après-midi d'un faune* (1912). Year 2 students focus on four mainstream modern dance works such as Graham's *Appalachian Spring* (1944) and Cohan's *Stabat Mater* (1975) and perform fairly lengthy excerpts from them. Year 3 students work on current artists such as Bausch in order to reconstruct her work and then to construct their own works in her style. They complete their studies by performing an entire work based on current dance theatre repertoire. All of this practical work is supported by student research, analysis and interpretation of the works studied through a range of resources including books, notation, music scores, choreographer's notes (where available) critics' writings, programme notes, pictures and dancers' memoirs.

• *Naturalism and Expressionism in Dance* are studied both practically and theoretically to develop students' understanding of these cultural practices. Naturalistic and expressionistic dance vocabulary and choreographic devices are analysed, compared and contrasted in a range of choreographers' works. Students are assessed through an essay and presentation of a practical performance which demonstrates appropriate selection and treatment of a theme and use of naturalistic/expressionistic procedures.

• *Dance on Film and Television and Dance Politics* are level 3 theory modules. These two separate modules build on and employ the year 2 theoretical approaches' content. The former uses the theoretical bases to analyse and understand dance on film and television as part of cultural practice. The latter applies social theory approaches to explore issues such as funding, policy-making, education and training in relation to a variety of dance 'institutions', particularly dance companies.

• *Period Study theory modules over three years* take a chronological and thematic route through the histories of dance and drama. Students study and compare traditions, modern and post-modern developments in both art forms, from the mid nineteenth century to the present day.

• *Theatre Techniques modules in year 2* aim to develop students' understanding and practical abilities in staging dance and drama performances in terms of lighting, sound and design.

• *Aesthetics and Culture theory is studied by all year 1 dance and drama students.* This is a basic philosophical course which considers concepts of dance, drama, art, expression, form, creativity, aesthetic experience and aesthetic judgement, and then requires students to take a critical stance on these aesthetic concepts taking account of Marxist views of art, class, mass audience and consumer culture. This introduces students to level 2 work.

• *Theoretical Approaches is an appropriate title for the level 2 compulsory theory module* in that a range of critical approaches – semiotic, psychoanalytic, feminist, poststructuralist – are employed to analyse how meanings are culturally produced in dance and drama 'texts'. Students are required to apply semiotic analysis techniques to a performance to decode the meanings produced. They learn that meanings are never stable but change and shift through time and in reception by different audiences. Dances and plays are decoded to discern ideologies and politics relating to sex, gender, class and race as features evident in today's cultural practices.

Ways in which the above example of dance practice implements the theoretical basis of the *midway* model

The above example of practice in higher education is examined below to substantiate the claim that it amalgamates some of the elements of the *educational* and *professional* models and incorporates many of the new aspects of the *midway* model for the art of dance in education as defined in chapter 1 of this book. It is hoped also that such an analysis of the art of dance in higher education will expose elements of good practice which, if fully understood, can be further developed to improve and enhance future practice.

The dance content described above clearly puts emphasis on experience of dances: choreographing, performing, viewing and appreciating them through practical and theoretical study from a range of different perspectives. Although there are modules which obviously focus on each of these strands, there is constant interdependency between them.

In choreography modules, for example, students learn as much from viewing the works of others (their peers and professional choreographers) and performing in each other's dances as they do from choreographing dances themselves. Also, in reconstruction workshop modules, where the emphasis is on performance, it is necessary to view, thoroughly to analyse, understand and appreciate the choreography in order to perform it well.

In both these examples and compared with secondary school practice, there is greater emphasis on study of professional exemplars and developing knowledge and understanding of the practices in professional choreography and performance to inform students' own work. This suggests that on a continuum between the *educational* and *professional* models, the art of dance in higher education is located much closer to the *professional* extreme.

Nonetheless, as will become clear below, there is evidence of some of the *educational* model's processes and practices in the art of dance in higher education. These should be retained and developed further in order that the *midway* model becomes established and extended as good practice in dance in this sector. This is more desirable than attempting to provide a totally *professional* (conservatoire) course in mainstream higher education institutions. Without the full diet of daily classes and specially selected students, such an attempt would probably produce second-class results.

1. Equal emphasis on process and product

In 'good practice' in the *midway* model for the art of dance in higher education, there is rather more emphasis on process than would appear. In all aspects of the above outlined modules, it is important that students become thoroughly knowledgeable about and understand the processes involved in creating, performing, viewing, appreciating, describing, analysing, interpreting and evaluating the dance movements and/or dances they experience.

In *technique and performance modules*, for example, students engage in analysis of and come to understand the principles and kinesthetic processes involved in the movements skills that they learn. Consideration of correct posture, placement, balance and anatomical functioning of the body helps students to acquire and improve dance skills. Similarly, understanding of elements of dance movement such as use of breath, accent, weight/gravity, rhythm, line, alignment, extension, tension and relaxation promotes improved performance of dance skills and dances. In determining the processes involved, it is also necessary to study the principles and concepts underlying the particular technique.

In Graham technique, for example, it is imperative that students understand principles of contraction and release which are concepts related to exhalation and inhalation, and also the processes involved in attaining the feeling of the movements in somewhere near the way Graham intended. Students should come to understand that there are three corollaries to this central principle: first, that dance movement should originate and be controlled from the centre of the body which, it is believed, has more emotional impact than peripheral movement; second, that breathing as a basis implies phrasing of movements into 'sentences' rather than a series of skills; and, third, that contraction and release connote introversion and extroversion qualities of movement. There are three other important principles to be considered in the study and practice of Graham technique. One is concerned with the opposition of forces, either in the body itself with parts moving in opposition or in the body in relation to gravity. Another is concerned with space and emphasis on the floor area and low-level movement. Yet another is concerned with rhythm in which the percussive or primitive beating quality is distinctive. Knowledge and understanding of all four principles, through feeling them in the moving body, viewing others employing them in performance, reading and writing about them and applying this knowledge in acquiring and improving Graham-based skills, constitute an important part of the process of learning Graham-based technique and performing Graham-based studies and dances. This kind of teaching/learning puts an emphasis on coming to know the processes in the movements themselves and, at the same time, engaging in the process of learning how to perform them successfully.

A very different approach is often adopted in a more professionally oriented training. Here, the movements are prescribed by the teacher (expert), directly taught and repeatedly practised by students (apprentices). Corrections are given, of course, but these are often accompanied by demonstration so that students have a visual (rather than cognitive) model of what is to be achieved. If movements are broken down, they are usually practised as separate parts which are gradually put together into a whole again. For example, a turning step pattern with accompanying arm and body co-ordinations might well be split into just the steps, then the arm and body movements, then these amalgamated and the turn added later. Such an approach is common in dance classes in higher education where the emphasis is on acquisition of the skills to be practised as products of the dance classes. Certainly, students need to acquire skills and abilities in order to combine and perform them as products of technique and performance classes. Moreover, it is not helpful to students aiming for performance assessments if too much emphasis is put on developing understanding of the processes. No matter how well the processes are understood theoretically, the practical realisation of this understanding resides in a quality product – the skilled performance. What is needed, of course, is a balance between the two approaches with an equal emphasis on process and product.

In *choreography modules* process is definitely as important as product. Throughout the above outlined modules, students are encouraged to explore, improvise, research for themselves and experiment with new procedures in order to inform their choreographic endeavours. These processes require individual imaginative flair (to be discussed below) and this cannot be produced to order. Students need to work on choreographic projects in their own time to become immersed in the processes of creative production. After research and experimentation there needs to be a time for reflection and imaginative thinking centred on the particular choreographic problem. The processes of selection, development and refinement of content then take place. During this time the students develop feelings towards the evolving choreography. They can hate it and discard it or feel good and excited about it and continue, even if they know that it needs a lot of work to get it right. There is rarely an indifference about it. These personal feelings are essential in creative work. This engagement – an interaction between the evolving choreography and the creator – is an aspect of the art of dance model which is missing from primary and secondary dance education (except perhaps for examination students). Higher education students have the luxury of time outside lectures to enjoy such processes.

Choreography lecture time then is not necessarily focused on personal creative responses. Rather, in my view, the lecturer might best consider this an opportunity to introduce or consolidate knowledge of principles and practices in choreography. For example, in a study of orchestration of motifs for a large group in a mainstream contemporary dance, students may be guided to view Jiri Kylian's *Symphony of Psalms*, the epitome of brilliance in this respect, and then, having identified some ways of orchestrating a motif, the students can practise this for themselves. Lecture time is also an important feedback and sharing time. In the context of viewing each other's choreographic products, students can learn not only about the choreography as an outcome that shows, for example, clarity of intention, originality in interpretation of the theme and treatment of content, depth in development of the motifs and richness in orchestration, but also about the processes that led to this product. Here, discussion and introspective thought on the processes involved, help the students to understand more about them.

If the 'journey' is as important as the 'arrival', understanding the nature of both is relevant in a *midway* model.

Further discussion can clarify how process plays a role in other modules, e.g. reconstruction workshop modules where 'getting inside' the work to be performed requires students to attempt to understand the motivations behind the work and the procedures employed in creating the work, in so far as these can be discerned by analysis of the work itself or other sources. Such analysis can be likened to analysis of literary texts to appreciate the author's uses of language in transmitting the ideas and images.

Suffice it to say that learning about and through qualitative processes, even in essay writing, will surely provide the possibility of qualitative products.

2. Equal emphasis on development of creativity, imagination and individuality, and an acquisition of knowledge of theatre dance

It has already been suggested above that students in higher education have the time, opportunity and capacities to develop their potential to be creative and imaginative in responding to choreography assignments. By this stage in their dance education, they do not need the security of a teacher's framework within which they choreograph their own movements (except perhaps at the beginning of the first year). Rather, they need a carefully-designed exposure to principles and practices in choreography and tasks which are sufficiently structured but which allow freedom of interpretation and choice in response to them. For example, current year 1 students at the end of the first term were required to complete the task on page 145 of my book *Dance Composition* (1992).

The task uses analysis of the beginning of Bruce's *Intimate Pages* to discern the richness in use of relationship possibilities for two bodies and the use of time to express feelings between the two dancers. The students were required to choose one of the titles – an argument – forbidden love – despondence or a related idea of their own and use music selected for them. The limits of the task above provided sufficient security in that a title was offered and there were numerous relationship possibilities provided through analysis of the video snippet. Yet there was much freedom to interpret the title in their own way, to select from the video any three duo relationships and create as many of their own as they liked, to use time aspects to express in their own ways and above all to select actions, spatial and dynamic content without restriction. The best outcomes showed imagination, creativity and individuality and at the same time showed what the students had learned about principles and practices in choreography in the first eight weeks of the module. They had:

- devised original motifs, abstracting from non verbal communication and symbolising in dance terms,
- repeated, developed and varied them,
- designed at least one contrast in the duo,
- created an overall unity of form,
- used a full range of duo relationship possibilities,
- used qualities of time to give expression to their movements,
- used the music in many different ways (a lecture had been devoted to this),
- interpreted the theme imaginatively, and
- communicated the expression clearly.

This list of attributes more than fulfilled the criteria in respect of showing knowledge of principles and practices in theatre dance choreography. The best outcomes achieved high marks. However, duos with few signs of imagination, creativity and individuality scored average marks even if there was evidence of all the above listed criteria. They lacked originality, freshness, distinctiveness, excitement, aesthetic interest – they were more predictable and 'academically sound'. Through discussion, it is possible to educate the students to distinguish the original and creative from the sound and 'safe' responses to tasks.

Choreography experiences in higher education are an obvious

context in which the duality discussed here should occur. However, as all dancers, actors and musicians would endorse, there is as much creativity, imagination and individuality required in the interpretation of a role/text/score as there is in creating one. In each excerpt performed by the students in *reconstruction workshop* contexts, there is room for them to be creative, imaginative and individual in applying the understanding they have gained through theoretical study of the dance work and analysis of it in video performances. Critical study of the piece will develop an in-depth appreciation of it and, if the student's performance is based on this without any limitations on interpretation being imposed by the lecturer, there is ample opportunity for creativity, imagination and individuality to play important roles in making decisions on how to express and perform the content of the reconstructed excerpt.

This implies a less didactic approach to teaching reconstruction workshops than would be perhaps expected. A more detailed discussion of methods of teaching that encourage a freer interpretive response from students is presented in (5) below. It is perhaps sufficient to say here that students should be given room for such freedom in the use of their imagination and creativity, especially as they progress from year 1 to year 3.

Learning about theatre dance is, of course, an essential aim for students in higher education. In all the above modules, there will be constant reference to theatre dance exemplars. Not only is this the case in choreography and reconstruction workshop modules, it is also extremely important in *period study, naturalism and expressionism, theatre techniques, aesthetics and culture* and *theoretical approaches*. In these modules, examples of period, style, expression, form, symbolism, semiotics, etc. need to be drawn from theatre dance traditions/conventions and current practices. Video resources have become principal means but artists in residence/workshops and frequent theatre visits are also essential if students are to develop knowledge and understanding of the art of dance in contemporary culture.

Again, 'good practice' in the art of dance provides an even diet of both opportunity to allow the students' creativity, imagination and individuality to develop and opportunity to gain a great deal of knowledge from theatre dance. The former ensures that the limitations do not restrict individuality and originality and that the learned 'rules' or guiding principles are broken, changed or abandoned and replaced with new ones as the students progress through their art of dance experiences. The latter ensures that students grasp the criteria of validity and value in dance and set their own originality and imagination against a background of the traditions and limitations of the art form itself. (See Bests's (1985) quotation on page 9.)

3. Equal emphasis on feelings and on training

It is important to ensure that the students' feelings can enter and play an essential role in successful learning in the art of dance. This is particularly the case in choreography, of course, where students create dances based on their own ideas, working through the processes from conception to realisation. Given a task such as this year 2 assignment:

Compose a group dance for 4–5 dancers. The dance should be based on a current cultural issue.

Students have a great deal of opportunity to work on themes about which they feel strongly. They are encouraged to start from their own feelings and explore ways in which these feelings can be expressed in dance movement. However, they will learn, if they do not know already, that their own strong feelings alone are insufficient bases upon which to build a dance.

There is no one way to proceed but it is certain that if the feelings are to be communicated through the medium of dance, knowledge of public conventions and shared meanings must also shape the outcome. Students need to research the topic and make decisions on how it should be treated. In doing this, they may make reference to ways in which professional choreographers have treated the same or similar topics and employ a few strategies gleaned from such sources. However, in order that their own feelings enter the work, it is important that they are not too strongly influenced by such references.

Students will have learned how to strip down an idea and symbolise its essence, how to stylise movements, how to create form and they may also have studied various choreographers' procedures, e.g. Cunningham's chance strategies. All of this knowledge is brought into the creative process but it is to be hoped that by the end of the second year, this knowledge will have been absorbed and become a part of students' intuition.

When can a student choreograph without consciously thinking about principles and methods? There should be a time within the higher education experience of choreography when the student feels confident that, in starting from feeling and strong motivation to create, the dance will evolve and develop almost entirely through intuition. Of course, intuition in this context refers to knowledge gained and absorbed into the subconscious without conscious thinking processes being involved. (See chapter 1 page 13.)

When a dance has been composed, there may well be an objective evaluation of it when knowledge is employed almost as a checklist (criteria of assessment can be used at this juncture) in order to make refinements. There should be a fairly flexible shift between feeling/subjectivity and knowledge/objectivity during the choreographic processes.

In *technique and performance* modules where clear objective ends are predetermined, there may appear to be less room for feelings and subjectivity to be involved in learning how to dance. However, as made clear in (1) above, if students do not inject feeling into their dance performance, it will remain mechanical and uninspiring to watch.

The feeling discussed here, however, is not the same as life feelings, e.g. sadness or anger, nor is it the same as those related to a theme for choreography as above, e.g. feelings evoked by the topic of marital rape. Rather, it is feeling intrinsic to the movements themselves, such as the feeling of openness, giving, indulgence and freedom in an upwards extending release, or the feeling of exhilaration in fast travelling and leaping actions, or the soft quiet closing of the body in hugging knees slowly in a sitting position. These sensory qualities need to be felt. The movements should have life and light and shade.

This sort of feeling can enter the movements only by means of the students' subjective commitment. This has erroneously been labelled 'sincerity' but, in my view, it is an attribute which can be achieved once the students are comfortable with the skills or dance sequences, provided that they are encouraged to enter into the feeling of the sensations intrinsic to the movements.

Hence, in a technique class, once the skills themselves are mastered, there should be a shift towards developing the ability of students to project the feelings in the movements when they perform them.

In *reconstruction workshop*, both the feeling sensations in the movements and the expressive meanings they evoke need to be felt by the student performing the excerpt. If there is no feeling, the student has little chance of conveying the idea of the dance. Again then, once the skills have been mastered and the student understands the choreography – phrasing, rhythm, timing, spatial and dynamic aspects, focus, expressive intentions and so on – 'getting inside' the choreography requires that students enter into the feelings it contains and express them when performing the piece.

Even in more academic situations, such as seminars in aesthetic theory related to dance, students should be encouraged to express what they feel about a topic and back it up from their own experiences. This may be stretching the point but, all too often, lectures are treated as information-giving events and seminars as smaller versions of the same thing. In any context, students will learn more if they become subjectively involved. Having received lectures and read about the concepts of classicism and romanticism, for example, students could view and analyse a dance work such as *Swan Lake* and then discuss ways in which it reflects these concepts. Here, students' own interpretations can be extended by listening to the views of others and the lecturer's input may well become the richer through discussion of alternative ideas which had not been thought of in preparation of the topic.

In conclusion then, it would appear that in the art of dance in higher education there should be emphasis both on feelings – subjectivity of experience and on objective ends. However, the module content will dictate the balance. Equal emphasis should be strived for in choreography and ultimately in performance contexts, too. Moreover, in interpretation of dances viewed in the theatre or on video there should always be a feeling response, preferably before detailed analysis takes place. The latter can sometimes hamper the former.

In summary, it may be fruitful to keep in mind the following proverb:

> Tell me and I will forget,
> Show me and I may remember,
> Involve me and I will surely learn.

4. Equal emphasis on movement principles and on stylised techniques

In higher education there is a good deal more time to devote to the learning of defined dance techniques than there is in secondary education. As stated in chapter 1 of this book, a comprehensive art of dance education will include study of a range of dance techniques so that the students have extended repertoires of content from which to select for choreographic and performance purposes.

A range of different styles opens up expressive possibilities far beyond the restrictions of one style. (See page 126 for discussion of the Graham technique in this context.)

This is the reason for selection of different contemporary styles in the *technique and performance modules* above. Each style has its own expressive boundaries and its particular vocabulary. Put them together, and the student has an extended vocabulary. However, learning just one technique and achieving a degree of expertise in performing it takes time. Learning three or four techniques over three years permits perhaps only a superficial knowledge and modicum of skill in each of them. Yet, as stated above, students need a more extended vocabulary than one technique allows, even if it is studied in depth. So, what is the answer to this problem?

The teaching of defined dance techniques in the conventional and conservatoire manner for a period of two hours (numerous exercises which carefully build co-ordination, strength, mobility, balance, extension, elevation and so on) has little relevance in higher education contexts, unless there is provision for daily classes in technique and further classes in performance. However, technique and performance modules have to cover both these aspects of dance study and there is no provision for daily classes. Even so, students can and do reach high standards in technique and performance. The route is merely a different one.

Certainly, techniques need to be taught through the careful build-up of appropriate dance exercises and sequences devised for teaching the skills. In a Graham class, for example, students will learn some of the floor exercises, centre practice, travelling movements and falls. However, each class, in my view, should contain a long sequence, style study or dance which combines movements into phrases and contrasting sections in the style of the technique. A technical or style study lasting about three minutes (see page 92) reduces much of the repeating and perfecting of exercises before such dance sequences are taught, the procedure practised in a conservatoire training. There is no time for this approach in other higher education institutions.

Teaching stylistically-defined techniques through dance studies permits technique and performance to be taught simultaneously. A good study will challenge the most able and be within the reach of the least able (the most complex parts can be simplified). It will include a variety of technical skills and emphasise the style of the technique. It will require the students to focus on performance skills such as dynamic variation, rhythm, projection, focus, alignment, spatial accuracy and expression. The study should be a formed coherent whole and students should learn how to dance it showing awareness of phrases, sections, transitions, contrasts and climaxes.

This approach in the teaching of technique through pre-choreographed studies/dances provides students with vocabularies of individual dance skills (for example, different travelling steps across the room from the corner) and, at the same time, demonstrates ways in which movements can be put together into stylised phrases and dances. Students are therefore learning to dance through dances.

This is also the case if they take *reconstruction workshop modules* in which they also learn a range of dance movements within styles – the style of the technique used by the choreographer and the style of the choreographer. For instance, in learning excerpts from *Dark Elegies* (1937), students would be learning some modern ballet technique in the style of Antony Tudor. In addition, students often have opportunities to extend their own technical dance skill and stylistic vocabularies through performing in other students' dances. First-year students, for example, can gain much from dancing in third-year pieces. Often there are individual students with particular expertise who, if given the opportunity to choreograph or teach open classes, can extend the students' experiences even further. This year has seen an input of street jazz and lindy hop and in former years there have been Alexander technique, S. Asian dance, Chinese dance, to name but a few. The opportunities outlined above are limited to practical experience. It is possible, of course, through study of developments and changes in dance works in modules such as *period study* and *naturalism and expressionism* to become acquainted with other stylistically-defined dance techniques (e.g. classical ballet) through viewing it and learning about it theoretically.

There is a range of opportunities for students to gain knowledge, understanding and a fair degree of skill in a variety of stylistically-defined dance techniques. It is important that students become familiar with a range of publicly-defined dance techniques. Since this is the 'language' of the art form, they need to know at least a part of it and should become skilful in using its specific terminology and concepts.

Students in higher education also need to know and understand movement principles such as those defined by Laban. As indicated throughout the book so far, this descriptive analysis of movement is invaluable as a flexible and comprehensive framework which can be used in both practical and theoretical contexts.

It remains an essential tool for choreography. It can be used to define tasks, to explore movement ideas, to describe and discuss movement, to guide observations of movement, to frame checklists for evaluation of movement.

In defining tasks, the movement principles themselves can be explored. For example, the concept of flow or continuity can be explored to discern the range of sensory and expressive qualities involved in moving freely and continuously, hesitantly, in a held-back manner, with sudden stops, with staccato quality, going and stopping and so on. If every aspect of the analysis were to be used as a starting point for such explorations of dance content, students would be exposed to a far wider range of expressive possibilities than would be the case if their dance experiences were limited to learning prescribed techniques.

In exploring movement ideas for choreography, students could identify the type of movement – for example, high extended jumps – and then try out variations by adjusting body shapes through positioning of the limbs, etc. The movement principles provide different possibilities within each movement concept Once motifs have been created, knowledge of the movement principles provides a framework within which students can try in different ways to develop or vary the content of the motif, through change of level, direction, quality of movement, addition of action etc. (See *Dance Composition*, 1992.)

Laban's framework also provides a checklist for use in observation, description, analysis and evaluation of dance content. Students can be guided to observe and discuss the actions: qualities of time, force and continuity; spatial aspects such as size, level, direction, pathway; and relationship features – dancers relating to others, to objects, to the audience. These movement principles together with knowledge of stylistically-defined dance techniques provide students with an extensive and comprehensive repertoire of concepts and terminology for use in observing, describing, analysing and evaluating dance content.

In the *midway* art of dance model, higher education students should gain knowledge and understanding, and acquire dance skills through experience of both a range of prescribed dance techniques and a set of movement principles, such as that defined by Laban. The former needs to be more emphasised than in secondary education but not to the detriment of limiting the students to the very specific boundaries of content that each dance technique prescribes. The latter should act as a frame of reference for the full range of dance content both within and beyond the defined techniques. It constitutes a generalised vocabulary of movement and language within which the specific technical content can be embraced.

5. Equal emphasis on problem solving and on directed teaching

In most discipline areas, students at this level certainly have to become more autonomous in their learning. In the performing arts, however, there is still the strongly–held view that students require more rather than less practical contact time with lecturers. With continual cuts in contact time, it has become a major battle to retain the additional hours required for practical modules. Arguments for favourable treatment in terms of hours and staff-student ratios have to be strongly supported by educational reasons if they are to be acknowledged by managers of timetables and funding. Perhaps there needs to be some re-thinking about the balance between student-based and lecturer-based teaching/learning.

In my view, all the above-named modules, except *technique and performance modules*, emphasise the problem-solving, student-based learning approach. In *choreography modules*, for example, the weighting of directed lecturer input is minimal in comparison to problem-solving tasks. In the majority of choreography contexts the lecturer acts as catalyst while the students are agents in their own learning. This is not surprising, of course, because students are the creators and have to be active rather than passive learners.

Reconstruction workshops are different in that the lecturer, especially at first-year level, teaches the students the content of the excerpts. Nevertheless, this direct teaching of movement content is only a first step in students coming to know, understand and gain skill in performance of the excerpt. The students have to 'make it their own' through research, reading, discussion, many viewings of professional performances of the excerpts and practice of its content. All of this work to 'get inside' the excerpts can be student-based. Practice should always take place outside lecture time so that lectures are used for input of additional content, for sharing information gained from students' research and for monitoring and evaluating performances in progress. In this context too, weighting is towards student-centred learning.

Theoretical modules, as for other subjects in degree courses, require students to put in at least twice the allotted lecture time for their own thinking, researching, reading and writing work. In dance, most theoretical modules require students to view work on video or in live theatre contexts and to spend time after the performance in reflecting on and writing notes or reviews to support their learning. Here again, there is more time spent in student-centred learning than in lectures but, even in the latter, there is a tendency to provide frameworks, principles and ideas which are then discussed by the students in lectures and seminars. It is through these opportunities in lecture time that students test the knowledge they have gained through research/reading/viewing tasks against that of their peers and the lecturer. Hence, lectures sometimes, and seminars always, need to be student rather than lecturer-centred.

Technique and performance modules remain the only ones which would appear to require a lecturer-centred approach. Certainly, in the *professional* model it is still a dominant practice to have the instructor in front of the students, often demonstrating the movements before teaching them. The class members are often positioned in formal lines and the instructor dictates what they should do, when they should do it, where and with whom it should take place. There is nothing wrong with this method especially if the teacher is an expert. It can be a very rewarding experience and it is a means of students experiencing the discipline needed to acquire skilled dance performance. However, such classes will not achieve all of the objectives for modules whose focus is on performance as well as technique.

While there needs to be some emphasis on process, there must also be emphasis on feelings and subjectivity if the students performances are to be given life. These qualities cannot be imposed; they need to be gained by the students through their own efforts. Moreover, if the students learn stylistically-defined techniques through technical/style studies, they may benefit from the approach outlined above for the learning of excerpts in reconstruction workshops. The difference, of course, lies in the fact that it is likely that the lecturer will have choreographed the workshop studies and therefore can and should take the role of expert more frequently while the students perfect it.

Students in higher education should progressively develop into independent, autonomous learners. They need in-depth information from lecturers some of the time but need them mostly to guide, inspire and provide feedback for their own learning.

6. Artistic education

All of the content discussed above constitutes artistic learning in that, through every experience in every module students will learn more about the art form of dance, mostly through the study of dances, creating, performing, viewing and appreciating them.

Current practice in the art of dance for university students makes constant cross reference between the students' own work and the public world of dance. The range of dance works studied, from the conventional classical ballet (period study) to the experimental post-modern (period study, choreography, reconstruction work-shop, naturalism expressionism, dance on film and television), exposes students to a plethora of dance movement, approaches to choreography, styles, themes, design aspects, accompaniments and approaches to audiences.

Concepts of what a dance is will be extended, challenged and changed. Experience of many dance works emanating from different eras, in different styles and performed in different contexts for different purposes, will provide examples of changes in principles, practices and conventions underpinning the art form of dance. Students will learn that concepts are never static and that, in common with all art forms, dance and dances are constantly changing.

Rather than reiterate the above text with a different emphasis, it seems sensible to redraw the essential content of artistic education for students in higher education in an extended form of the list in chapter 1.

Artistic learning through:

Choreographing dances

• understanding of and interpretation of themes/ideas especially those relating to contemporary issues
• translation of the themes/ideas in dance terms, i.e. into symbolic action employing a range of different strategies and conventions – traditional approaches, e.g. naturalism and expressionism, abstraction into symbolism, formalism; post-modern approaches, e.g. chance, minimalism, deconstruction, use of pedestrian movement
• making decisions about the type of dance, e.g. dramatic, pure, comic, abstract and the style, e.g. mainstream/traditional, contemporary, post-modern or new dance in style, balletic, jazzy, street dance flavoured, social or ethnic dance styles – pure or mixed

• exploring movement ideas discovering actions, qualities, rhythmic and spatial features to express the theme in the type and style of dance planned: knowledge of stylistically-defined dance techniques balanced with knowledge of a set of movement principles should be employed in the search for new content
• exploring and making decisions about the numbers of dancers, gender, and the relationship possibilities between them to express the idea, e.g. positioning, group shapes, orchestration, contact/ non-contact,. etc.
• understanding of how the music or accompaniment can be used: students in higher education should experience making their own music/sound tracks at least once
• selecting and linking of movements to make motifs and phrases
• stylising of content appropriately, considering the choreographic conventions/approaches, type of dance and overall style
• deciding on the order of the movements and refining motifs and phrases, again considering the above
• structuring the motifs and phrases in time, space and the relationship between the dancers
• developing the phrases, perhaps repeating them in time, space and relationship configurations
• understanding and use of formal devices: repetition, development, variation, contrast, transition, climax, logical progression, unity or alternative construction processes such as chance
• creating sections/parts of the dance and relating them to make whole dances
• considering and planning staging aspects of dances: lighting, design, costume, make-up, use of accompanying visual/audio materials, etc.
• rehearsing of dancers to achieve the expression
• presenting dances in conventional/alternative spaces with consideration of the role of the audience (programme notes etc.)

Performing dances

• acquiring of appropriate physical skills: actions combined with dynamic, rhythmic and spatial patterning or stylistically-defined skills from specific techniques
• performing the above with co-ordination, accuracy, fluency, control, balance, poise and authority
• practising of the co-ordinations that link movements into phrases, sections and dances

• performing the content concentrating on qualitative expression through variation of dynamic, spatial and relationship features
• performing dances and parts of dances with understanding of the formal qualities, e.g. pauses, highlights, contrasts
• presentation of the theme through dancing with appropriate expressive intention
• practising to music or other forms of accompaniment alone or with others in unison and canon
• developing performance qualities such as extension, projection and focus to express meaning
• concentration on line, body shape, clarity of design, positioning
• clarity and unity of style.

Viewing dances

• all the above aspects involved in creating and performing dances should be observed, described, analysed, interpreted and evaluated by students viewing their own and professional choreography throughout their dance education.

These three processes – creating, performing and viewing dances – will culminate in the development of ability to appreciate artistic features of dances.

Appreciation of artistic aspects of dances

• students will learn to discern with increasing accuracy and sensitivity a range of qualities in choreography and performance. From their own experiences in choreography and performance and through learning how to employ description, analysis, interpretation and evaluation, they will be able to perceive distinctive artistic features: style, form, expression, techniques and production.
• in order to further appreciation, students will learn to employ a range of resources to discover background information and specific details about dances, choreographers, performers, designers, musicians, etc.
• students will gradually adopt a number of theoretical perspectives with which to view artistic content, devices and meaning, and performance, e.g. history, semiotics, aesthetics, cultural studies.

7. Aesthetic education

Aesthetic education through dance occurs in a number of different ways in choreographing, performing and appreciating dances. All of the discussion in chapter 3 relating to aesthetic education of secondary pupils through dance experiences pertains here. However, students in higher education know and understand in a distinctly different way what may constitute the aesthetic in a dance and the nature of aesthetic experiences.

In studying the art of dance in higher education, it is essential that students gain knowledge of aesthetic theory relating to dance. This area of study as a branch of philosophy is essentially discursive. There are no right or wrong answers, rather there are concepts, and arguments supporting or negating those concepts. Students need to consider various writers' views in order to determine their own on the following concepts:

• the nature of art, the art of dance, a dance as an art object, intentions and expectations
• expression in art – imagination, creativity and individuation in art – art and artistic traditions
• form in art
• concepts of beauty, meaning and truth in art
• aesthetic experience, aesthetic qualities in art and outside art, aesthetic criteria and judgments
• aesthetic criticism, interpretation and evaluation.

Having studied such aesthetic concepts, students may well become more open to and able to perceive the aesthetic dimensions of dance works, their own, those of their peers and those professionally choreographed and performed. Their discussion as to why they like or dislike a dance should become much more informed in that they can point out the excellence or otherwise, using aesthetic criteria and terminology.

Students, for example, can employ the aesthetic framework discussed in chapter 1 which was defined by Osborne (1970) referring to the sensory, expressive and formal qualities in the dance/object perceived or, having studied alternatives, they may prefer to employ, for example, Beardsley's framework of general canons which can be used in making aesthetic judgments in art. Beardsley suggests that merits or demerits can be ascribed to works of art in relation to the canons of unity, complexity and intensity. The canon of unity is employed when an art work is described as well organised (or poorly organised), formally perfect (or flawed) or to have (or lack) a logical pattern, coherence of style and structure. The canon of complexity relates to statements such as – the work is well developed, rich in contrasts and variety (or lacks variety and is dull) it articulates the theme in depth and with subtlety (or it is banal and crude). The canon of intensity relates to the human regional qualities or feelings contained in the piece i.e. the dramatic, vital, forceful, tender, tragic, delicate, comic qualities (as opposed to objects lacking expressiveness which could be labelled insipid or pale). Moreover, Beardsley suggests that experience of viewing an art work that has these qualities would afford the perceiver an experience which can also be qualified as aesthetic in that it is unified, complex (deep) and intense (absorbing and feelingful).

Students with this knowledge and understanding have invaluable devices for making and understanding the different kinds of judgments that can be made about art works and the types of reasons given to support the judgments. They can also set this aesthetic discussion about dance and dances against other theoretical approaches used to discuss, interpret and evaluate art. (Some of these approaches are described under the heading of 'cultural education' below.)

The difficulty of ensuring that the students' dance education contributes to their aesthetic education lies in the fact that different lecturers teach them different aspects of the course. Hence, tutors who deliver *technique and performance modules*, for instance, may not be conversant with the aesthetic concept of the sensory, expressive and formal qualities contained in the movements and may, therefore, not be able to help students perceive the qualities kinesthetically in their own movements or visually in others' performances. It is encumbent upon the students themselves to make such links though, in ideal circumstances, the theory and practice should merge if references are made to both by the two sets of tutors. Similar comments could be made about the students' work in choreography and in reconstruction workshop, where aesthetic perception of the dances as art works is imperative if the students' dance experiences are to be labelled study of the art of dance.

Every experience of choreographing, performing and viewing dances should have potential for developing the students' aesthetic experience and appreciation. Theatre visits and work with dance artists are particularly advantageous in this respect except that, as yet, it is often difficult for students to gain aesthetic insight into the artists' work because the artists do not have the concepts or language with which they can share such insights.

This constitutes a gap in the theory of dance practice *per se* and has much to do with the distance between the two worlds of dance – the *educational* and *professional* worlds. Perhaps the growing popularity of resource-based teaching (see below) in the *midway* art of dance in education will force the two worlds to liaise and to learn from each other. Educationists are already learning from professional exemplars. It is the other way round that needs to be addressed so that the professional contribution of artists in schools projects is appropriately focused to enhance artistic and aesthetic education.

Students in higher education then, should both experience the aesthetic in dance and dances for themselves and come to know and understand the theory behind the practice. In this way, they could be described as aesthetically educated in both the subjective and objective senses.

8. Cultural education

The discussion in chapter 3 under the heading of cultural education is relevant here in so far as the students' experiences of creating, performing and viewing dances develops their understanding of concepts and practices underpinning the art of dance in Western culture. In higher education, however, such understanding could be endorsed and extended through application of new theoretical areas of study.

In the above-described example of dance in higher education, developing an understanding of the art of dance as part of contemporary culture is of paramount importance, hence the title of the programme within the BA degree, i.e. *Dance and Drama in Contemporary Culture*.

To this end, students study semiotics, the theory of signs. This is also described as structuralism in that the approach is based on analysis of dance works as texts which are organised like language with their own specific grammar and which can be read to reveal underlying deep structural significances. The signs within dance encode both general and dance-specific cultural meanings. This theoretical approach requires that students consider dances to be culturally-produced phenomena which can reveal psychological perspectives of the author/choreographer, ideologies, social values sexual politics and views pertaining to class, race and so on.

Cultural education must include consideration of dance works as reflecting the culture from which they derive and in which they are performed. (The latter requirement refers to works choreographed long ago because they will probably reflect something of the culture from which they emerged and much of the culture in which they are being interpreted and recreated for performance.)

In study of dance from a cultural perspective, students should also come to realise that culture itself is a constantly shifting and changing social process in which all meanings relate to the various social systems that exert influence on its products. This kind of study is forever on shifting sands.

Moreover, it tends not to consider the art work itself because it focuses outwards on the social conditions of production.

This theoretical approach offers students an antithesis or opposing argument to the concept of the art of dance having aesthetic purpose. Of course, students could argue against cultural theoretical perspectives and be in favour of applying aesthetic and artistic criteria in discussion of art. Clearly, they should understand and be conversant with these differing points of view.

History is a further essential theoretical study of the art of dance. Concepts such as classicism, neo-classicism, romanticism, modernism and post-modernism need to be understood in both their historical and cultural contexts. Study of dance history provides a theoretical framework within which students come to understand traditions, conventions and changes in practices of choreography and performance.

Through the study of dance as a cultural/historical phenomenon, students learn that there is no such thing as constant aesthetic meaning in art works. In this climate of changing meanings, students come to understand that concepts of expression and form in art are also open to challenge and that post-modern artists or those described as avant garde will continue to experiment with these concepts to produce new and shifting boundaries. What counts as art is therefore ever changing.

The aim of this kind of cultural education is to ensure that students leave university with an open mind and a readiness to discuss and challenge constraining or restricting views of the art of dance. Students with an open mind in these respects are more likely to promote shifts and changes in their future practices in the art form of dance.

In the *midway* model, cultural, historical and aesthetic theoretical perspectives provide conceptual bases for the study of dance in higher education in that all of the theory develops greater knowledge and understanding of the art of dance itself and its works as cultural, historical and aesthetic phenomena. This is different from the approach in the early 1970s when discipline areas loosely related to dance were studied for purposes of making dance a respectable degree study. There was very little reference and application to dance but today theory is always supported by and applied to dance; theory informs practice and practice informs theory. Without use of video resources and theatre visits this would be very difficult. References create the links between theory and practice. Dance works, and choreography and performance practices, in the professional public dance world merge with educational concepts and practices to create what can be called a *midway* art of dance model in higher education. On a continuum between the *professional* and *educational* models for dance in education, the model for higher education would probably be placed much closer to the professional end in terms of content but close to the educational end for methodology. The result is perhaps more *midway* than might be expected.

RESOURCE-BASED TEACHING/LEARNING

Resources in the form of dance works on video or better still through live performances are central in study of the art of dance in higher education. The content in each section of this book headed 'resource-based teaching/learning' can be applied to higher education in that there is constant use of resources to support students' work in choreography, performance and appreciation: artistic, aesthetic, cultural and historical. However, there is a difference between using such resources as references or stimuli for practical and/or theoretical dance study and resource-based teaching/learning through resource packs. At present, the latter is not a developed feature of dance courses in higher education.

In BEd degrees and in postgraduate certificate of education courses, the practice of devising resource packs for teaching GCSE/AS/A level students has been in place for some years. In these school or further education college based courses however, dance teachers are usually responsible for the whole course and time is allocated to dance overall rather than to specific dance activities: technique and performance, choreography, etc. This might make it easier to teach through a resource pack which, according to the rationale given in chapter 1, should address all three strands: creating, performing and appreciating dances (the latter including historical and contextual study). In colleges of higher education, however, courses are taught by several different lecturers and content is split into separately-assessed modules. So what role can resource packs take in higher education?

Resource packs are certainly needed for dance in higher education. The students might then be able to advance their own learning in a truly student-centred manner. Perhaps, this 'open university' approach will catch on in the event of even further cuts in time, lengths of academic year and degree courses overall. Even if time allocation remains the same, there are distinct advantages in making resource packs available to students.

Resource packs[1] for further and higher education – a prescription for future practice

Resource packs can be based on any aspect of dance study. It would be most advantageous, for example, if the lecturer concerned with period study could direct the students to use a resource pack on, say, romantic ballet. The pack could contain a video or, better still, an interactive video compact disc[2] on which snippets of romantic ballet works would be interspersed with text on screen, voice-overs or reference to readings in books or within the pack booklet itself. Pictures, photographed programmes and posters, etc. and questions based on the reading and viewing tasks given in the carefully-sequenced programme of learning could also be contained in the pack. (A compact disc could offer the student a number of different levels and routes through the content which has a distinct advantage over the linear approach necessarily taken in VHS video production). In effect, the resource pack can replace lecture preparation. The lecturer need no longer spend endless hours of sorting and editing appropriate video snippets (if available) and photographing slides from books in order to deliver information on romantic ballet. How much better it would be to have a really good resource bank of such learning materials on a single compact disc and spend the lecturer's time with the students in deep debate on the topic after

(1) See chapter 1 pages 43–4 for a description of what a resource pack might contain.
(2) Interactive video is computer-controlled video. The video images are pressed onto a disc which is digitally read by means of a computer. It is possible to jump from place to place on the disc at a touch of a button or mouse, to have more than one image on screen and to overlay the picture with simultaneous moving graphics, text and voice overs.

they have gained the essential information and understood the concepts through use of the pack.

For the teaching of all the modules described above, especially practical modules, resource packs devised to structure students' learning could be extremely advantageous. Each pack would be the equivalent of several brilliantly-delivered lectures but students would use them on a one-to-one basis and could go back over bits of information, play some of the video snippets again to capture the detail, listen to the music accompanying the dance work under scrutiny, read passages again and relate them to the viewing tasks, and so on. Students could even learn short excerpts of the work/s to exemplify a particular point. This would certainly be beneficial in choreography, technique and performance modules, whilst in reconstruction modules it is of central concern.

All of these instances attempt to demonstrate the benefits of resource packs in student-centred learning. Resource packs take students much further than reading books or listening to lectures. Of course, this is due to the fact that the student-based learning involved in using the packs requires a student's active response to the practical, viewing, reading, listening, discussing tasks as he/she progresses through the pack. (See example outline for a resource pack on page 209 in the appendix).

A resource pack for teaching dance technique and performance would seem to negate the claim above that it remains the single area of dance study which requires more rather than less lecturer input. However, rather than replace the lecturer in this context, a resource pack could speed up and enhance the students' learning of technique and performance. This is illustrated in the example in the appendix where an interactive video resource pack aiming to teach a GCSE technical study is described in detail. If such resource packs were available for teaching, say, Graham technique, students could advance their learning by leaps and bounds in that it would be like having master classes at one's finger tips on numerous occasions.

Imagine for instance, having superbly-performed floorwork exercises on screen during lectures. This immediately frees the lecturer to observe and comment on the students' attempts. Then imagine that students have use of the interactive video disc between lectures in order to perfect their skills through access to a detailed and slow-motion breakdown of the actions involved. The disc would provide notation, anatomical or kinesiological input if required, audio teaching points, information about the co-ordinations, dynamics, rhythm, spatial patterning, use of breath involved in the movements, and so on. This kind of resource would surely improve skill acquisition in the same or similar ways employed in individual tutorials. Furthermore, additional content on the interactive video disc might go on to develop the students' performance abilities through overlay graphics, notation, voice-overs, shots of the movements from different angles, slow motion, freeze frame options, etc. to focus on qualitative features such as variation of dynamics, fluency, line, focus, projection, expression and a sense of form in performing the piece.

Through publication of packs such as those outlined above and perhaps numerous other packs on choreography, through which students could study particular choreographic procedures, individual choreographers or groups of choreographers, resource-based teaching/learning is becoming an important method for the art of dance in higher education in the future.

Conclusion

Throughout this book the *midway* art of dance model has promoted a multi-dimensional approach in that it is strongly contended that all three strands (creating, performing and appreciating) are experienced as interdependent. Higher education is no exception. Even though the content is split into separate modules with an emphasis on performance rather than choreography, it all builds towards in-depth appreciation of the art of dance. Creating, performing and appreciating dances permeate the modular programme described in this chapter.

The model described can justifiably be claimed as a *midway* model in that there is evidence of elements of both the *professional* and *educational* models, albeit much altered through time. There is also evidence to support the view that the art of dance in higher education contributes towards artistic, aesthetic, and cultural education and employs a modified form of resource-based teaching.

Conclusion

Chapters 2, 3 and 4 have demonstrated the inextricable relationships between current good practice and the theory expounded in chapter 1 for the *midway* model of the art of dance in education.

The distinctive features of this model are important in dance experiences in all sectors – primary, secondary and higher education. These are:

a) the three processes, creating, performing and appreciating;

b) emphasis on dances;

c) the education that these lead to – artistic, aesthetic, cultural.

This book has defined the distinctiveness of the *midway* model in the above terms and in terms of a combination of aspects from two opposing models to warrant the title of *midway* model for the art of dance in education. The degrees to which each sector employs these aspects can be illustrated thus:

Features retained from the **educational** *and* **professional** *models*

EDUCATIONAL MODEL	PROFESSIONAL MODEL
Emphasis on the process	Emphasis on the product
Emphasis on development of creativity, imagination and individuality	Emphasis on knowledge of theatre dance as the model towards which to aspire
Emphasis on feelings – subjectivity of experience	Emphasis on objective ends, e.g. trained bodies for performance of dances
Emphasis on a set of principles as a source of content	Emphasis on stylistically-defined dance techniques as content
Emphasis on a problem-solving approach to teaching: teacher as guide, pupil as agent in own learning	Emphasis on directed teaching: teacher as expert, pupil as apprentice

THE ART OF DANCE IN EDUCATION *MIDWAY* MODEL

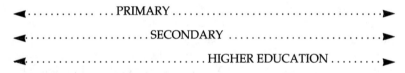

This is an attempt to show the different emphases put on the retained aspects of the *educational* and *professional* models by primary, secondary and higher education practitioners respectively. It therefore identifies differences in interpretation of the *midway* model in the varying educational contexts.

The feature not listed above but which has been discussed in all three contexts as an essential means of delivering qualitative learning experiences in the art of dance in education, is resource-based teaching/learning. Whilst access to live dance performances must remain at the top of the priority list in the art of dance in education, the essential back-up resources, especially video recordings, are very sparse indeed.

It is surely time that dance teachers, in common with other arts teachers (music, art, drama and poetry, for example) could borrow videos and accompanying materials from a library of resources to support the content of lessons/lectures. Although there is a growing number of videos available for purchase, contemporary dance videos are very scarce.

There is much to be achieved by the provision of such resources and some dance companies are responding to the need by producing their own dance packs. However, these packs do not yet contain the comprehensiveness, level or depth of treatment of topics needed, especially for A level courses and beyond. Moreover, packs that contain a linear video combined with notes, books, slides, literature, pictures, worksheets, etc. are becoming outmoded now that interactive video is on the market.

Interactive video is computer-controlled video. A compact disc can store a wealth of information including video images. It is possible to jump from place to place at the touch of a button, the screen or mouse, and to have more than one picture on screen at once with overlays, voice-overs and notation. The next two or three years will see the arrival of compact interactive video equipment in schools and colleges. This is a very cheap system for the users. However, it is of no use to dance teachers until there is a bank of quality resources from which to choose.*

Resource packs containing compact video discs and other materials for the study of choreographers' works, particular techniques/styles of dance, historical developments, design and dance, etc., will in future provide a much-needed library of resource materials for teaching the art of dance in education at all levels. This future is on the horizon and the *midway* model of the art of dance in education will become further established as access to resource materials improves.

Dance Laser Disc 1 was produced in 1989 by the author and Schofield, J. If funding permits it is planned to publish in 1994–5 an interactive video resource pack based on a work choreographed by Siobhan Davies.

⟶

The Art of Dance in Education – Some Guidelines for Primary and Secondary Teachers

Content of this appendix

The intention here is to offer teachers guidance where there is a lack of literature at present.

To date, in the context of dance in the National Curriculum, there has been very little guidance as to how the few sentences (components) in each programme of study specific to dance can be interpreted. The National Curriculum Council's *Physical Education Non-Statutory Guidance* (1992) had failed to deliver in this respect and the Arts Council's *Education — Dance in Schools* (1993) booklet had no such brief. The intention of the latter was to *provide a framework for debate, a starting point for teachers, governors, advisers, those involved in teacher education and INSET* on what constitutes dance in education. As might be expected, partnership between education and dance artists is a strong feature in this booklet but it is also very helpful in providing clear guiding principles on why dance should be taught and what is dance, and on how the dance curriculum-policy can be put into practice. There are short sections on equal opportunities, special needs, gender, cultural diversity and careers in dance. As a policy document for dance in schools for teachers and for those concerned in teacher education, particularly for key stages 1 and 2, this is helpful, but detailed interpretation of the programmes of study for dance is not yet available.

The following pages provide primary and secondary teachers with a comprehensive interpretation of the programmes of study for dance contained in the 1992 Order for *Physical Education in the National Curriculum* where a few sentences count as programmes of study. The National Dance Teachers' Association's *Dance Matters*, a twelve-page termly paper, contains lesson materials and ideas for teachers, but these few centre pages can only briefly address all age ranges.

In my view, in order to achieve the fundamental principle of entitlement for all, there should be a move towards consensus in interpretation of the new national guidelines for dance in education. The interpretations of programmes of study offered in this book may provide a start in development of shared understanding on what constitutes content for the art of dance in education. From this beginning there are bound to be changes and it is to be hoped that these will be instigated by the teachers who experience delivering dance in the National Curriculum. Indeed, changes are already imminent as a result of the Dearing recommendations. However, these proposals will not be confirmed until the end of September 1994 and will not be sent to the schools until January 1995. (The School Curriculum and Assessment Authority *Draft Proposals for Physical Education*, May 1994, do not imply enormous changes for dance. The wording of the content for dance is almost exactly the same although some of the sentences have been combined and the content for key stage 3 has been divided into two units. The end of key stage statements are also much the same in the draft proposals although again separate sentences have been combined.)

In the light of the above, a comprehensive interpretation of the 1992 programmes of study content for dance is still very much needed. It must be made clear, however, that this is an entirely personal interpretation of the dance content implied for each key stage. As they stand at present, the statutory programmes of study for dance and other aspects of physical education constitute flexible frameworks within which teachers should work. Moreover, to date, no assessment criteria have been published to guide teachers on content, levels or standards of achievement. The end of key stage statements are also open to interpretation. Consequently there is still much freedom implicit in interpretation of dance in the National Curriculum.

This appendix also contains detailed lesson content for the dance outcomes discussed in chapters 2 and 3. As teachers read the relevant chapters they can make reference to this detailed planning to help them apply theory to the practical teaching situation. Although it is not expected that teachers will prepare in as much detail, the principles underpinning good planning for dance lessons should emerge and guide teachers in their planning.

In addition to these detailed lesson contents, some alternative dance frameworks are offered for different year groups, followed by lists of learning activities taken out of the relevant programmes of study.

For teachers of GCSE, a technical study resource pack is described in order to demonstrate the range of learning outcomes that can be derived from such a resource. Following this, a sample A level resource pack is described to illustrate the values of this methodology in the *midway* art of dance model.

Programmes of study for dance

For the purposes of providing comprehensive interpretation of the programmes of study and in order that readers can discern progression through all the key stages, a detailed breakdown of each of the components of the programmes of study into learning activities and learning outcomes is presented on separate pages. It will be noted that examples of content are directly related to the *midway* art of dance model.

Progression should be considered as a spiral in that earlier key stages should be revisited on a regular basis as indicated below.

KEY STAGE 1	KEY STAGE 2	KEY STAGE 3	KEY STAGE 4
PoS 1 ....▶................▶..............▶.........▶			
	PoS 2 ....▶..............▶.........▶		
		PoS 3 ....▶.........▶	
			PoS4 ....▶

To give a complete picture, the programmes of study and end of key stage statements are presented in advance of the detailed interpretations of each component of the programmes of study. The latter have been re-ordered and given headings. These identify the focus of each component and indicate progression between the key stages.

KEY STAGE 1	KEY STAGE 2	KEY STAGE 3	KEY STAGE 4

DANCE ACTIONS ....
EXPRESSIVE FEATURES OF DANCE ....
EXPRESSIONS IN DANCE ....
MAKING DANCES ....

DANCE COMPOSITION

USE OF ACCOMPANIMENT ....

PERFORMING SET DANCES

DANCE APPRECIATION

Physical Education in the National Curriculum, programmes of study for dance key stages 1 & 2

KEY STAGE 1 DANCE: Pupils should:	KEY STAGE 2 DANCE: Pupils should:

DANCE ACTIONS

• experience and develop control, co-ordination, balance, poise and elevation in basic actions including travelling, jumping, turning, gesture and stillness.

• be given opportunities to increase the range and complexity of body actions, including step patterns and use of body parts.

EXPRESSIVE FEATURES OF DANCE

• explore contrasts of speed, tension, continuity, shape, size, direction and level and describe what they have done.
• be helped to develop rhythmic responses.

• be guided to enrich their movements by varying shape, size, direction, level, speed, tension and continuity.

EXPRESSIONS IN DANCE

• experience working with a range and variety of contrasting stimuli, including music.
• be given opportunities to explore moods and feelings through spontaneous responses and through structured tasks.

• in response to a range of stimuli, express feelings, moods and ideas and create simple characters and narratives in movement.

MAKING DANCES

• experience and be guided towards making dances with clear beginnings, middles and ends.

• make dances with clear beginnings, middles and ends involving, improvising, exploring, selecting and refining content, and sometimes incorporating work from other aspects of the curriculum, in particular music, art and drama.
• describe and interpret different elements of a dance.

The programmes of study above are statutory and should be taught in order that end of key stage statements can be reported. The end of key stage statements indicate the skills, knowledge and understanding that should be achieved in physical education overall. Specific reference to skills, knowledge and understanding pertinent to dance is minimal but there are many ways in which they can be implemented through dance. Guidance on application of the dance programmes of study for key stages 1 and 2 has been given in chapter 2. The content of these is reiterated below.

Physical Education in the National Curriculum

END OF KEY STAGE STATEMENTS KS1	END OF KEY STAGE STATEMENTS KS2
By the end of the KS pupils should be able to:	By the end of the KS pupils should be able to:
a) plan and perform safely a range of simple actions & linked movements in response to given tasks & stimuli.	a) plan, practise, improve & remember more complex sequences of movement.
b) practise and improve their performance.	b) perform effectively in activities requiring quick decision making.
c) describe what they and others are doing.	c) respond safely, alone & with others, to challenging tasks, taking account of levels of skill and understanding.
d) recognise the effects of physical activity on their bodies.	d) evaluate how well they & others perform & behave against criteria suggested by the teacher and suggest ways of improving performance.
	e) sustain energetic activity over appropriate periods of time in a range of physical activities & understand the effects of exercise on the body.
	Physical Education in the National Curriculum DES April 1992

Detailed interpretations of the programmes of study for key stages 1 and 2 are presented on the following pages. End of key stages statements are applied to the interpretations.

KEY STAGE 1

Individually and when ready in pairs and in small groups, with or without accompaniment and through different DANCES pupils should:

- *experience and develop control, co-ordination, balance, poise and elevation in basic body actions including travelling, jumping, turning, gesture and stillness.*

DANCE ACTIONS

LEARNING ACTIVITIES

- movements of the whole body – stretch, curl, twist and different body parts – head, trunk, legs, arms, shoulders, elbows, wrists, hands, fingers, hips, knees, ankles, feet, toes - moving independently, taking weight or leading.
- travelling actions – walk, run, skip, crawl, stagger, slide, creep, rush, stride, march, prance, prowl, jog, dodge, trot, gallop.
- jumping actions – jumping from 2 feet to 2 feet, 1 to the same (hop) 1 to the other (spring or leap).
- turning actions – spin, whirl, spiral, roll.
- gestures – movements of free body parts, e.g. arms, legs, shoulders (includes everyday non-verbal communication like waving and shrugging; work actions like digging and sweeping; and symbolic dance gestures like stretched arms high to express elation or arm punch with closed fist to indicate anger).
- stillness – stop, freeze, balance, hold, hesitate, pause, settle.

LEARNING OUTCOMES

CREATING – pupils should be led to:
- respond spontaneously and to improvise to stimuli and/or accompaniment emphasising particular body parts or actions or showing a variety of actions according to the task.
- explore, discover, select and refine dance actions suitable for the dances they experience.
- create their own actions and action phrases and remember and repeat them in the dances they experience.

PERFORMING – pupils should be led to:
- isolate and use all body parts separately and in simple co-ordinations (e.g. arms swinging with legs marching).
- be able to control their bodies in balances, elevations and in moving in the space.
- stand/sit well with poise and move with ease to change body shapes/positions.
- be able to perform the actions listed above separately and in simple sequences (e.g. travel into jump and hold still).
- practise and improve the clarity of and quality in actions (e.g. extension in jumping and resilience in landing) and dance them with confidence and co-ordination.

APPRECIATING – pupils should be led to:
- name all body parts and describe the movements they do with them.
- name and describe the actions they and other dancers perform.
- suggest meanings implicit in actions they experience in dance (e.g. dragging feet and sad, miserable feeling).

END OF KEY STAGE STATEMENTS (see page 157)
All statements – a) b) c) and d) – are applicable to the above learning outcomes.

KEY STAGE 1

Individually and when ready, in pairs and in small groups, with or without accompaniment and through different DANCES pupils should:

- *explore contrasts of speed, tension, continuity, shape, size, direction and level and describe what they have done – be helped to develop rhythmic responses.*

EXPRESSIVE FEATURES OF DANCE

LEARNING ACTIVITIES

- vary actions through contrasts of speed – slow, fast, sudden, enduring.
- vary actions with degrees of tension – strong, light, forceful, gentle.
- vary actions with differences in continuity – flowing freely, hesitant, ongoing/continuous or stopping with ease, hesitant.
- use body shape and size – round, twisted, narrow, wide, small.
- use space around them and room space, directions – forward, backwards, sideways, up and down, levels – high, medium, low.
- use pathways on the floor – curved or straight, squares, circles, zig-zags.
- use pathways and shapes in the air – curved or straight – circles, squares, alphabet letters, numbers, etc.
- combine elements to create rhythmic patterns – accent, phrases, simple divisions of time (e.g. skipping, running, marching).

LEARNING OUTCOMES

CREATING – pupils should be led to:
- respond spontaneously and improvise with a variety of stimuli (music, sound, poetry, objects, etc.) using contrasts of speed, tension and continuity relevant to the task/idea.
- differentiate and select the above qualities appropriately in creating dance movements/phrases to express ideas, feelings/moods (e.g. sharp, strong, quick movements to depict lightning).
- vary the actions they select through changing direction, level, size and shape using their own and the general room space effectively.

- create floor and air patterns in response to tasks, e.g. travel in a circle and then draw a circle round your body.
- respond spontaneously and accurately to different rhythms and create movements showing awareness of them.

PERFORMING - pupils should be led to:
- perform actions with different qualities – speed, tension, continuity, and to contrast these qualities, e.g. change from slow to fast, strong to light.
- practise and improve the qualities in their movements and to show understanding of them as expressive features in dance.
- perform actions in different directions, levels and pathways showing awareness of size, shape and space around the body, in the room and in relation to others.
- dance rhythmically to a variety of music/stimuli showing awareness of accent, phrasing and simple time changes.

APPRECIATING - pupils should be led to:
- describe the qualities, rhythms and the spatial patterning in the actions they perform and see.
- interpret the kinds of meanings/feelings such qualities convey (e.g. fast, light, ongoing and large actions, on zig-zag pathways – for excitement) and evaluate the expressive features in their own and others' dance performances.

END OF KEY STAGE STATEMENTS (see page 157)
Statements b) and c) are applicable to the above outcomes.

KEY STAGE 1

Individually and when ready, in pairs and in small groups, with or without accompaniment and through different DANCES pupils should:

- *experience working with a range and variety of contrasting stimuli, including music.*
- *be given opportunities to explore moods and feelings through spontaneous responses and through structured tasks.*

EXPRESSION IN DANCE

LEARNING ACTIVITIES

- use of a range and variety of stimuli – stories, colours, patterns, sculptures, poems, pictures, natural phenomena, objects, shapes, etc.
- experience of a range of music as both stimuli and accompaniments – different in type (classical, folk, percussion, electronic, etc.) in rhythm, style, mood and instruments used.
- exploration of moods (happy, sad, calm, angry, etc.) of feelings/emotions (caring, proud, greedy, scared, etc.) in response to various stimuli (e.g. music) spontaneously and/or in structured tasks.

LEARNING OUTCOMES

CREATING – pupils should be led to:
- improvise and explore a range of actions, qualities and spatial features of dance in response to a variety of stimuli (e.g. cats provide a range of different actions – pouncing, creeping, arching, stretching, rolling, curling which can be performed with varying qualities of speed, tension and continuity in different directions, levels and pathways).
- improvise and explore a range of moods and feelings and the actions, qualities and spatial features of dance which express them (e.g. sad – subdued, heavy, slow steps, head lowered and sinking movements).
- in response to the teacher's structured task, select and create actions, qualities and spatial features appropriate to the stimulus and/or feeling/mood of the dance.

PERFORMING – pupils should be led to:
- use different kinds of accompaniment (music, poetry, percussion sounds) while dancing showing ability to listen and respond sensitively to it.
- dance with musicality aware of rhythm, tempo, beat and intensity.

APPRECIATING – pupils should be led to:
- describe simply the elements of the stimuli (e.g. the changes in a piece of music – slow quiet beginning, a loud fast middle section and repeat of the slow bit at the end; the colour contrasts in a picture; the movements of a cat)
- describe ways in which the stimuli suggest movements (e.g. the movement of the sea on the shore – forward and back gentle hand movements).
- interpret the expressive meanings/feelings in the stimuli they use and/or see in the dances of others.
- comment on the stimuli and their feelings about them (e.g. whether they like the music or not and why).

END OF KEY STAGE STATEMENTS (see page 157)
Statements b) and c) apply to the above outcomes.

KEY STAGE 1

Individually, in pairs and in small groups, with or without accompaniment and through different DANCES pupils should:

- *experience and be guided towards making dances with clear beginnings, middles and ends.*

MAKING DANCES

LEARNING ACTIVITIES

- respond to a stimulus to find movements.
- experiment and/or explore movement vocabulary – actions qualities, spatial and relationship features to express the idea, mood or feeling.
- select appropriate movement in response to structured tasks.
- refine movement content and repeat it accurately within the dance.
- structure the movements into dance phrases and sections within the teacher's framework, e.g. create a sequence of swinging movement to depict swings in a playground dance.
- find starting and ending positions appropriate to the theme.
- work alone, with a partner or in a small group to respond creatively to tasks set, e.g. having been led to explore turning actions with a partner they could make a sequence to depict roundabouts for the playground dance.
- match movement to accompaniment.
- perform the dances they make (normally based on the teacher's framework) showing an understanding of beginnings, middles and ends.
- with the teacher, plan frameworks for whole dances and (occasionally towards the end of the key stage) make short dances of their own – choosing theme, music/accompaniment and movements by themselves.

LEARNING OUTCOMES

CREATING – pupils should be led to:
- employ the above processes – exploring, selecting, refining, revising and repeating movements and sequences to make dances based on the teacher's frameworks.
- solve problems and make decisions on the appropriateness of movement in response to tasks.

- make individual and group responses to creative tasks using their own ideas;
- develop concepts of form through considering how the parts of the dances – beginnings, middles and ends – relate to make whole dances.

PERFORMING – pupils should be led to:
- remember the order of parts of dances.
- show clarity in starting and ending positions.
- dance expressively to show understanding of meaning.
- practise and improve whole dance performances to accompaniments (if used).
- perform dances with awareness of other pupils in pairs or groups, taking turns or working in unison.

APPRECIATING – pupils should be led to:
- describe in simple terms the content, accompaniment and structure of the dances they experience.
- interpret the meanings in dances they make or see.
- comment on the dances they make or see looking for beginnings, middles and ends.
- begin to discern different types of dances, e.g. dramatic, lyrical and styles of dance, e.g. folk and social.

END OF KEY STAGE STATEMENTS (see page 157)
Statements a) b) and c) apply to these learning outcomes.

KEY STAGE 2

Individually, in pairs, in small groups and (with teacher guidance) in larger groups, with or without accompaniment and through different DANCES pupils should:

- *be given opportunities to increase the range and complexity of body actions, including step patterns and use of body parts.*

DANCE ACTIONS

LEARNING ACTIVITIES

- combine and isolate two or three moving parts of the body in simple co-ordinations, e.g. head, arm and leg movements (robot dance).
- discover different ways of performing each body action, e.g. extending the vocabulary of jumps to include one to two feet and two to one foot, travelling on different body parts, turning part of the body (twist), turning in different amounts (half, quarter, 2) and in a variety of ways (spiralling, hopping, stepping).
- combine actions, e.g. travel and gesture, turning jumps, travelling turns (rolls), travelling turning jumps.
- perform step patterns – e.g. 4 walks, 4 skips, 8 gallops.
- combine step patterns with other body actions, e.g. in a dance about making friends, the above travelling step pattern could be performed twice to find a partner (chorus), then together the children could perform a jumping sequence (verse), the step pattern could then be repeated to find a new partner and a turning sequence could be performed.

LEARNING OUTCOMES

CREATING – pupils should be led to:
- improvise and explore actions to create a range of appropriate vocabulary for each of the dances they experience.
- explore and discover ways in which actions can be linked and combined to create action phrases and step patterns.
- select appropriate actions and use of body parts in relation to the themes of dances and accompaniment used.

PERFORMING – pupils should be led to:
• perform sequences of actions with control, co-ordination, balance, poise and elevation.
• practise and improve precision, clarity and quality in use of body parts in combination and in performance of actions separately and/or in combination.
• perform actions rhythmically and expressively in relation to dance themes and accompaniment.
• perform actions in relationship with other dancers in unison and canon with appropriate timing and spacing.

APPRECIATING – pupils should be led to:
• describe and comment on appropriateness, range, variety, originality of body actions and use of body parts in dances they create and perform and/or dances they see (e.g. videos of professional dances).
• observe, describe accurately (sometimes in writing) and evaluate sequences of actions performed by themselves or others.
• appreciate the meanings implicit in dance actions.

END OF KEY STAGE STATEMENTS (see page 157)
Statements a) b) c) e) and f) are applicable to the above outcomes.

KEY STAGE 2

Individually, in pairs, in small groups and (with teacher guidance) in larger groups, with or without accompaniment and through different DANCES pupils should:

• *be guided to enrich their movements by varying shape, size, direction, level, speed, tension and continuity.*

EXPRESSIVE FEATURES OF DANCE

LEARNING ACTIVITIES

• combine separate qualities, e.g. strong and fast or gentle and slow – with a range of actions.
• make gradual or sudden changes of speed, tension and continuity using a range of actions.
• show clarity of shape, direction, level and size in performing different actions.
• understand and use qualitative and spatial elements as expressive features of dance.
• develop greater sensitivity to rhythm and rhythmic changes.

LEARNING OUTCOMES

CREATING – pupils should be led to:
• improvise, explore and select from separate and combined qualities - speed, tension and continuity - to colour their actions and to express feelings/moods/ideas.
• pattern their movements in space paying attention to size, level, direction, shape and pathway according to the expressive intentions (e.g. large, high, stretched movements travelling forward on a straight pathway to convey aggression).
• use a range of different stimuli – music, poetry, pictures, etc., to discover how the qualitative and spatial features they contain stimulate dance expression (e.g. strong, gushing, sweeping music with changes in pitch up and down might be appropriate for a windy day dance; a Lowry painting might stimulate different rhythmic working actions and group walking patterns in hunched up body shapes).

PERFORMING – pupils should be led to:
• practise and improve actions with contrasting qualities (e.g. fast then slow), combining qualities (e.g. fast and strong), and gradually changing qualities (e.g. accelerate/decelerate).
• show clarity in body shape, size, level, direction and pathway of movement.
• enrich their expressive performances paying attention to the above qualities and spatial features.
• develop further their ability to dance using more complex rhythms and variations of phrasing (e.g. Vivaldi's *Les Quatre Saisons*).

APPRECIATING – pupils should be led to:
• describe changes in qualities of speed, tension and continuity, and in rhythmic and spatial patterning in the dances they perform and see.
• interpret the qualitative and spatial features of dance to suggest expressive meanings.
• evaluate the qualities and spatial features in their own and others' performances.

END OF KEY STAGE STATEMENTS (see page 157)
Statements a) and e) are applicable to the above outcomes.

KEY STAGE 2

Individually, in pairs, in small groups and (with teacher guidance) in larger groups, with or without accompaniment and through different DANCES pupils should:

- *in response to a range of stimuli, express feelings, moods and ideas and create simple characters and narratives in movements.*

EXPRESSION IN DANCE

LEARNING ACTIVITIES

- extend the range of stimuli used as a basis for dance and develop responses to more mature/complex ideas sometimes linked to other aspects of the curriculum (e.g. ideas might include – electricity, magnetism, war, green issues such as deforestation, football, etc.).
- give more detailed attention to music – its qualities (e.g. crescendo/diminuendo – getting louder/getting softer, staccato/legato – sharp, clipped and separated/smooth continuous and linked), style (full and romantic; precise, symmetric and classical; rhythmic, fluid and folky; rhythmic beaty and jazzy), form (e.g. repeated passages, build-ups and climaxes; verse and chorus; ABA), its rhythmic patterns (accented sounds, phrases with `commas' and `full stops'; its time signature and tempo).
- experience further creating and performing dances based on moods and feelings taking more responsibility in choice of actions, qualities, spatial and relationship features to express them.
- study character and dramatic action between characters and ways of expressing these in dance (e.g. Scrooge-like mean and greedy actions would include grabbing, gathering towards oneself, pushing away movements which could cause cowering reactions from Bob Cratchit).

LEARNING OUTCOMES

CREATING – pupils should be led to:
- improvise and explore a range of movements combining actions, qualities, spatial and relationship elements in

response to the more complex stimuli – ideas, poems, music, pictures, natural phenomena, etc.
- through sensitive response in movement, show more understanding and knowledge of elements of music and create sequences which complement the music used.
- discover and select for themselves a range of actions, qualities, spatial and relationship features which depict mood, feeling, idea (e.g. earthquake) character and dramatic events (e.g. quarrelling).

PERFORMING – pupils should be led to:
- practise and improve their dance movement so that it effectively reflects the stimulus (e.g. volcano actions need to be explosive, strong, energetic).
- perform to music with a developing awareness of its features and show this in movement (e.g. pauses, climaxes).
- perform characterisations and dramatic interaction with expressive clarity.

APPRECIATING – pupils should be led to:
- interpret the meanings/feelings in the stimuli and offer their opinions as to how they might be used in dance.
- use increasingly elaborated language, including metaphors, to describe the stimuli/moods/feelings/characters and narratives and the movement which depicts them.
- comment on the stimuli and the dance outcomes and offer their opinion of them.

END OF KEY STAGE STATEMENTS (see page 157)
Statements a) and e) are applicable to the above outcomes.

KEY STAGE 2

Individually, in pairs, in small groups and (with teacher guidance) in larger groups, with or without accompaniment and through different DANCES pupils should:

- *make dances with clear beginnings, middles and ends involving improvising, exploring, selecting and refining content, and sometimes, incorporating work from other aspects of the curriculum, in particular music, art and drama.*

MAKING DANCES

LEARNING ACTIVITIES

- improvise freely and within structured tasks.
- explore and find new and different ways to answer tasks.
- select appoopriate answers in movement to creative problems.
- refine and rehearse movements, sections and whole dances which can then be repeated.
- experience further aspects of group work in dances, e.g. negotiating, planning, selecting, composing.
- use other aspects of the curriculum to illustrate structural aspects of dances, e.g. rhythmic patterns, lines and verses in poetry, life cycles in natural phenomena like a thunderstorm, volcano, day and night, musical structures, etc.
- find language, including metaphors, to describe movement, to interpet meanings and to evaluate the structure of dances they make or see.

LEARNING OUTCOMES

CREATING – pupils should be led to:
- find a greater range of responses in improvising, exploring, selecting, and refining movements and sequences to make dances based on teacher's frameworks.
- structure phrases and sections of dances and with help from the teacher, plan and make whole dances.
- work on tasks independently – individually, in pairs and in small groups, and, with help, in larger groups.
- use aspects of partner of group work to express ideas, e.g. mirroring, leading and following, copying, contrasting, moving in unison, in canon, making group shapes – lines, circles, clusters.

- make links between other aspects of the curriculum and the dances they make – thematic links or conceptual, e.g. comparing the structuring of stories and dances.

PERFORMING – pupils should be led to:
- remember, practise and perform dances they have made, sometimes over a period of time, e.g. possibly over 3–4 weeks and perhaps building a repertoire of dances.
- show greater awareness of structure of dances in their performances – beginnings, phrases, pauses, stops, sections, contrasts, climaxes and ends.
- develop performance skills in presenting dances to audiences – focus, projection, expression, dancing with others and with the music (if any).

APPRECIATING – pupils should be led to:
- describe and interpret the content of dances – actions, qualities, spatial and relationship aspects (what they see and what it means).
- describe and interpret the structure of dances – the phrases, the sections, beginnings, middles and ends (what happened as the dance progressed and where and why the different parts occurred).

END OF KEY STAGE STATEMENTS (see page 157)
Statements a) b) c) and e) are applicable to these learning outcomes.

Physical Education in the National Curriculum, programmes of study for dance key stages 3 & 4

KEY STAGE 3: DANCE
Pupils should:

KEY STAGE 4: DANCE
Pupils should:

DANCE COMPOSITION

• be taught how to develop and use appropriate methods of composition, styles and techniques to communicate meanings and ideas.

• be given opportunities to create dances which successfully communicate the artistic intention.
• be guided to devise and design aspects of production for their own compositions.

USE OF ACCOMPANIMENT

• be guided to create and perform short dances showing sensitivity to the style of accompaniment.

PERFORMING SET DANCES

• be taught to perform set dances, showing an understanding of style.

• be taught to perform complex and technically more demanding dances accurately and expressively.
• be given opportunities to dance in a range of styles showing understanding of form and content.

DANCE APPRECIATION

• be taught to support their own dance compositions with written and/or oral descriptions of their intentions and outcomes.
• be taught to describe, analyse and interpret dances recognising stylistic aspects of production and cultural/historical contexts.

• be guided to record the process of composition.
• be given opportunities to describe, interpret and evaluate all aspects of dance including choreography, performance, cultural and historical contexts and production.

NB The order of the above has been changed and headings have been added by the author

The end of key stage statements are indicative of the skills, knowledge and understanding to be achieved through the total physical education programme and so they are written in very general terms only. However, there are many ways in which they can be implemented through the dance programmes of study. The end of key stage statements are as follows:

Physical Education in the National Curriculum

END OF KEY STAGE STATEMENTS KS3	END OF KEY STAGE STATEMENTS KS4
By the end of the KS pupils should be able to:	By the end of the KS pupils should be able to:
a) devise and adapt strategies and tactics across appropriate activities within the programmes of study.	a) show increased knowledge, improved competence and safe performance in their selected activities.
b) adapt and refine existing skills and develop new skills safely across the activities in the programmes of study.	b) understand and take different roles in their selected activities.
c) practise and perform movement compositions devised by themselves and others in appropriate activities in the programmes of study.	c) develop and apply their own criteria for judging performance.
d) understand and evaluate how well they and others have achieved what they set out to do, appreciate strengths and weaknesses and suggest ways of improving.	d) prepare, carry out and monitor personal programmes for a healthy and enjoyable lifestyle, considering the use of community resources where appropriate.
e) understand the short and long-term effects of exercise on the body systems and decide where to focus their involvement in physical activity for a healthy and enjoyable lifestyle.	*Physical Education in the National Curriculum* DES April 1992

Detailed interpretations of each of the components of the programmes of study for key stages 3 and 4 are presented on the following pages. End of key stage statements are applied to the interpretations.

KEY STAGE 3

Individually, in pairs and in groups, with or without accompaniment and through different DANCES pupils should:

- *be taught how to develop and use appropriate methods of composition, styles and techniques to communicate meanings and ideas.*

DANCE COMPOSITION

LEARNING ACTIVITIES

- develop skills in researching/brainstorming ideas for dances.
- learn how to select and treat themes appropriately for dance.
- develop skills in selecting and using a range of different stimuli.
- explore, select, discard, refine action, dynamic, spatial and relationship content to communicate meanings and ideas.
- learn how to abstract and symbolise ideas.
- create motifs, develop and vary them.
- with increasing autonomy use composition methods of repetition, contrast and highlight/climax.
- extend abilities to create overall form – sections, transitions and unity.
- show understanding of relationship between themes of dances and styles.

LEARNING OUTCOMES

CREATING – pupils should be led to:
- discover, explore and improvise a range and combination of actions, dynamics, spatial and relationship content in response to varied stimuli to communicate meanings and ideas.
- discard, select and refine content from the above exploration and improvisation to create motifs.
- repeat content – exactly and through development.
- develop motifs and vary them with help from the teacher.
- use processes of abstraction to symbolise ideas.

- use a variety of ways of orchestrating in time and space for partner and group dances, e.g. use of canon, unison, spatial relationships, group shapes.
- structure phrases and sections of dances based on the teacher's framework and with increasing autonomy plan whole dances.
- work on tasks independently, in pairs, and in groups.
- stylise movements in relation to the theme.

PERFORMING – pupils should be led to:
- remember and perform the dances created and show understanding of the expression and form in the dance.
- perform sensitively with others in unison, canon and with spatial clarity.
- improve abilities to perform with stylistic coherence.

APPRECIATING - pupils should be led to:
- describe and comment on their own and others' choreography, including professional choreography in terms of appropriateness of content – actions, dynamics, spatial and relationship aspects and form – motifs, developments, contrast, climax, logical sequencing and overall unity.
- interpret meanings and ideas reflected in the choreography.
- discuss qualities in performance and ways in which it might be improved to serve the choreography.
- describe and comment on stylistic features of dances in relation to themes.

END OF KEY STAGE STATEMENTS (see page 175)
Statements a) c) and d) are applicable to the above learning outcomes.

KEY STAGE 3

Individually, in pairs and in groups, with or without accompaniment and through different DANCES pupils should:

- *be guided to create and perform short dances showing sensitivity to the style of accompaniment.*

USE OF ACCOMPANIMENT

LEARNING ACTIVITIES

- extend the range of accompaniment used for dances including music in different styles.
- continue to learn about constituent elements of music and how they can be employed in dance, e.g. rhythmic changes, key changes, accent, syncopation.
- explore the use of words accompanying music.
- study the use of different instruments and combinations of instruments, including human voices as stimuli for dances.
- study of different styles in musical accompaniment including a variety within each category of style, e.g. within classical music there are numerous styles differentiated through period, place and composer.
- use of accompaniment other than music, e.g. poems, narrative, sound effects.
- create short dances using accompaniment in different styles.

LEARNING OUTCOMES

CREATING – pupils should be led to:
- explore and compose dances/dance movements using a range of music accompaniment in different styles, e.g. classical, popular, jazz, and music of other cultures.
- show understanding of pitch, duration, rhythm, pace, key changes and dynamics in the music and ability to relate to or complement these elements of music with dance movement in composition contexts.
- discern character, mood or style of the music, effects of the above elements to create the character, mood or style and understand how these aspects in the music can be reflected in the movement, e.g. accent and syncopated beats in jazz, heavy, slow, deep, long sounds for sadness.
- discern structure or form in the music accompaniment and complement this with form elements in dance compositions, i.e. repetitions, contrasts, phrases and sections.

- use sound accompaniment other than music including words, everyday conversation and sound effects, e.g. wind, war sounds, marching feet, traffic, sea, breathing, heartbeat for dances.
- use songs or poems as accompaniment for dance, discover ways of relating dance movement to the words and the whole taking account of meaning and, rhythmic structure.

PERFORMING – pupils should be led to:
- show ability to perform dance movement and dances paying attention to constituent elements, character, mood, style in the music accompaniment, i.e. musicality.
- perform using a variety of music and sound accompaniment.
- show understanding of form of the accompaniment and the way it complements, contrasts with the form in the dance, e.g. demonstrate the 'commas', 'full stops' in phrases, contrasts and climaxes in overall form.

APPRECIATING – pupils should be led to:
- describe, interpret and evaluate all the above features of accompaniment and the effects it has in creating dances their own and professional dance works.
- describe, interpret and evaluate their own, each other's and professional dancers' performance in relation to the accompaniment used.

END OF KEY STAGE STATEMENTS (see page 175)
Statements a) b) c) and d) are applicable to the above learning outcomes

KEY STAGE 3

Individually, in pairs and in groups, through different DANCES pupils should:

- *be taught to perform set dances, showing an understanding of style.*

PERFORMING SET DANCES

LEARNING ACTIVITIES

- extend range of dance skills through learning set dances, particularly technical studies, i.e. pre-choreographed studies based on physically challenging movement content.
- extend vocabulary of dance content (movement principles and stylistically defined dance techniques) through learning their peers' and set dances.
- develop ability to stylise dance movement through performing style studies i.e. pre-choreographed studies which emphasise specific styles.
- develop knowledge of style through learning to perform a range of dances in different styles including those from different cultures.
- develop knowledge and understanding of stylistic characteristics of different genres – contemporary, ballet, jazz, African, Indian, English folk, etc., and styles within the genres.
- develop knowledge of factors affecting style – place, time, company, etc.
- learn aspects of form via experience of set dances as examples.

LEARNING OUTCOMES

CREATING – pupils should be led to:
- employ aspects of style in their own choreography appropriate to themes.
- extend knowledge of form through experience of pre-choreographed technical/style studies and through set dances, e.g. Israeli folk dances.

PERFORMING – pupils should be led to:
- develop and improve abilities to co-ordinate movements of parts of the body – in isolation, simultaneously, and in succession.

- develop abilities to control and co-ordinate movements of parts of the body in relation to other parts in static or travelling actions.
- improve balance, control, poise, mobility and strength of body for dance.
- extend range of travelling, jumping, turning, gesturing and balancing while still and combinations of these in sequences (movement principles).
- extend and improve abilities to show variations of quality in movement, i.e. speed, force, continuity, in rhythmic patterns (movement principles).
- extend and improve abilities to pattern actions in space using different and changing levels, directions, size, pathways, shapes (movement principles).
- develop and extend abilities to dance in relationship with other dancers in pairs, in groups varied in time-canon/ unison, and space-lines, circles, formations, etc. and in relation to objects, dance space and audience.
- learn some specific dance skills and vocabulary of stylistically defined dance techniques e.g. contemporary (generalised) jazz, African.
- learn how to stylise dance movement through performing style studies, i.e. studies in the style of specific genres (e.g. ballet, S. Asian), specific choreographers (e.g. Bruce, Davies, Anderson).
- develop range of vocabulary and style through performing excerpts or whole set dances from theatre and/or folk and/or social repertoires.

APPRECIATING – pupils should be led to:
- demonstrate knowledge and understanding of style through viewing, talking and writing about the stylistic features which differentiate dances in the above repertoires.
- demonstrate knowledge and understanding of how the stylistic features are derived through influences of period, place, groups and choreographers.
- show increased understanding and knowledge of specific dance techniques.

END OF KEY STAGE STATEMENTS (see page 175)
Statements a) b) c) d) e) are applicable to the above learning outcomes.

KEY STAGE 3

Individually, in pairs and in groups, through different
DANCES pupils should:

- *be taught to support their own dance compositions with
  written and/or oral descriptions of their intentions and
  outcomes.*
- *be taught to describe, analyse and interpret dances
  recognising stylistic differences, aspects of production and
  cultural/historical contexts.*

DANCE APPRECIATION

LEARNING ACTIVITIES

- learn how to describe ideas for dances verbally and in written
  form and how these have developed from the initial stimulus
  or starting point.
- learn how to describe the content of their own dances, those
  of their peers, professional dance works, social or folk dances,
  i.e. actions, qualities, spatial and relationship
  features and how these relate to the theme/type of dance.
- learn and use the appropriate technical language to describe
  types and styles of dances and specific technical dance
  vocabulary.
- describe accompaniments and production features of dances,
  i.e. costume, lighting, design, properties and comment on
  their relationship to themes.
- interpret meanings of dances using understanding of how
  moods, feelings and ideas are symbolically presented in
  dances.
- develop awareness of coherence in style and relationship of
  style to type of dance and techniques employed.
- develop abilities to record movement details including floor
  patterns, rhythm and group shapes, etc., using some form of
  notation, e.g. motif writing (Labanotation), stick figures or
  equivalent.
- begin to learn about cultural and historical contexts through
  experience of performing and viewing different styles of
  dances derived in different periods and places.

LEARNING OUTCOMES

CREATING – pupils should be led to:
- support their compositions orally or in writing by describing the stimuli, motivations, processes employed and reasons for choices.
- describe and analyse the content (actions, qualities, spatial and relationship features) and interpret meanings they perceive in their own and others' dance compositions.
- describe and analyse the form aspects in their own and others' dances.
- describe the use of style in relation to the ideas for their and others' dances.

PERFORMING – pupils should be led to:
- perform dances with a greater awareness of all the above features having described, analysed, interpreted and recorded them.

APPRECIATING – pupils should be led to:
- describe and analyse their own, their peers and professional dance outcomes in relation to intentions, content, form, accompaniment, and production elements verbally and in writing.
- interpret possible meanings in relation to the above and discuss these verbally or in writing.
- appreciate the relationships between all the above features and begin to comment on attributes such as originality, appropriateness and effect.
- make links between idea, type of dance, content, form, style, accompaniment, production elements and historical/ cultural contexts.

END OF KEY STAGE STATEMENTS (see page 175)
Statements c) (particularly PoS general statement 1) and d) apply.

KEY STAGE 4

Individually, in pairs and in groups with increasing autonomy, with or without accompaniment and through different DANCES pupils should:

- *be given opportunities to create dances which successfully communicate the artistic intention.*

- *be guided to devise and design aspects of production for their own compositions.* (This is highly unlikely to be extensive i n that lighting and staging items are not readily available in schools. It is therefore presented here as an extension to composition rather than an item in its own right.)

DANCE COMPOSITION

LEARNING ACTIVITIES

- extend skills in researching ideas and planning for dance compositions and select increasingly mature ideas e.g. social, environmental issues.
- plan dances individually, in groups and/or with the teacher and class.
- communicate intentions for dance compositions with increasing clarity.
- employ different starting points – ideas, movement, auditory stimuli, tactile including clothing, literature, poetry and visual stimuli.
- create different types of dances, e.g. comic, dramatic, abstract, pure.
- select accompaniments using a range of different types (music, poetry, sound effects, breathing etc.) in different styles and show understanding of constituents, mood, style of the accompaniment in relation to dances.
- select appropriate content to convey expressive intention – actions, qualities, spatial and relationship features including learned specific dance skills if appropriate (e.g. specific falls or contact work).
- stylise the content appropriately and coherently throughout dances.
- employ principles of form – motif, development, repetition, variation, contrast, transition, climax and unity in shaping dances with sections, linked into wholes.

- use methods of orchestration of the motifs – numerical variation, group shape, copying, complementing and contrasting, unison, canon, etc.
- consider audience in presentation of all the above – for example spatial placing, shape, line, focus and projection.
- rehearse dancers in appropriate space to improve presentation of dances showing clarity of intention.
- costume and make sets where appropriate and within minimal budgets.
- use lighting if available to enhance the intended communication.

LEARNING OUTCOMES

CREATING – pupils should be led to:
- select and research appropriate ideas for dances and plan outcomes individually or as part of a group demonstrating clarity of intention.
- select appropriate type of dance and accompaniment (if any) for idea and content/technique and style to convey the ideas.
- demonstrate understanding of principles of form and orchestration of dancers to convey the ideas.
- develop techniques of rehearsing dancers (especially if standing outside dances in the role of choreographer).
- develop understanding of aspects of production and how they can enhance the dance outcomes.

PERFORMING – pupils should be led to:
- perform the above dances conveying the intended expression and with an understanding of form, use of accompaniment, presentation elements, etc.

APPRECIATING – pupils should be led to:
- demonstrate knowledge and understanding of all the above elements.

END OF KEY STAGE STATEMENTS (see page 175)
Statements b) and c) are applicable to the above learning outcomes.

KEY STAGE 4

Individually, in pairs and in groups with increasing autonomy, with or without accompaniment and through different DANCES pupils should:

- *be taught to perform complex and technically more demanding dances accurately and expressively.*
- *be given opportunities to dance in a range of styles showing understanding of form and content.*

PERFORMING SET DANCES

LEARNING ACTIVITIES

- further extend skills through learning more complex set dances – technical studies, dances from different sources, e.g. teacher's choreography, peers' dances and snippets from professionally choreographed dance works.
- further develop dance vocabulary through the above and style studies, i.e within a particular style and using vocabulary specific to the style, e.g. a Cunningham study.
- develop abilities to perform accurately and remember dance movements linked into phrases, sections and whole dances showing understanding of expression and form.
- extend performance skills such as dynamic variation, focus, extension, line, projection, rhythmic accuracy and musicality.
- develop abilities to perform dances alone or as part of a group in a variety of contexts.
- extend knowledge of and ability to dance in a range of styles.

LEARNING OUTCOMES

CREATING – pupils should be led to:
- learn more about composition of dances through performing a range of well made dances and studies.
- learn more about style through experience of stylistically defined dances and studies.

PERFORMING – pupils should be led to:
- develop further their physical skills in co-ordination of body parts and combinations of actions simultaneously and successively.

- increase ability to demonstrate control, balance, poise, mobility, and strength in varieties of dance sequences.
- extend range and ways in which actions, qualities, and spatial patterning can be performed in isolation and in combination, e.g. different jumps and leaps alone and combined with turns and changes of direction.
- extend vocabulary and ability to perform stylistically defined dance techniques e.g., jazz and African dance steps and dances.
- demonstrate understanding of style through accurate use of body, rhythm, dynamics, weight, etc., e.g. jazz dance should show accented isolations particularly of hips and shoulders, syncopated rhythms, downward stressed grounded movements with sharp changes of direction and focus.
- show understanding of expression and form in dances, e.g. qualities of fast lightness emphasised to show liveliness contrasting with a section on slow, heavy and downward action to show sorrow – the ability to change moods and feelings within dances should be developed through such work.
- improve performance skills and abilities to dance solo and in groups.

APPRECIATING – pupils should be led to:
- increased knowledge and understanding of what constitutes skill in dance.
- increased knowledge of vocabulary for dance from experience of movement principles and selected stylistically defined techniques, e.g. Cunningham, jazz, African.
- learn more about style and processes of stylisation through performing and viewing dances including professionally choreographed dance works.

END OF KEY STAGE STATEMENTS (see page 175)
Statements a) and c) are applicable to the above learning outcomes.

KEY STAGE 4

Individually, in pairs and in groups with increasing autonomy, with or without accompaniment and through different DANCES pupils should:

- *be enabled to record the process of composition.*
- *be given opportunities to describe, interpret and evaluate all aspects of dance including choreography, performance, cultural and historical contexts and production.*

DANCE APPRECIATION

LEARNING ACTIVITIES

- identify different ways of recording movement, writing about it employing correct terminology, drawing figures, floor plans, group positions, etc., and employing simple notation symbols.
- learn how to record the processes of composition through journal keeping or other written forms including above to note initial stimulus, research, exploration of movement ideas, reasons for selection, process of refining motifs, developing them, etc., in order to give form to dances.
- write and talk about expressive and stylistic features of own dances.
- practise employing frameworks for description of choreography and performance, i.e. movement principles, composition principles, knowledge of types of dances, speci-fied dance styles, performance skills, production features, knowledge of history and cultural contexts of dances.
- learn how to employ descriptive language including metaphor to communicate interpretations of dances and to evaluate dances.

LEARNING OUTCOMES

CREATING – pupils should be led to:
- record, discuss and write about aspects of choreography listed on page 30 in chapter 1 of this book.

- learn more about choreography from this process of description, analysis, interpretation and evaluation of own dances, those composed by peers and professionally choreographed dances.
- use all the above knowledge to improve own choreography.

PERFORMING – pupils should be led to:
- record, discuss and write about aspects of performance listed on pages 30–1 in chapter 1 of this book.
- learn more about performance from the process of describing, analysing and evaluating own performances (through use of video), performances of peers and professional dancers.
- learn more about dances and different interpretations in performance of them by comparing the same dances performed by different people, companies or at different times.
- use all the above knowledge to improve own performances.

APPRECIATING – pupils should be led to:
- develop abilities to observe, describe, analyse, interpret and evaluate dances.
- develop ability to use language to describe content of dances and to convey meanings.
- extend range of specialised vocabulary to describe dance movement, techniques and styles.
- apply knowledge of dance composition and performance (checklists on page 30–1) in order to make informed evaluations of dances.
- apply knowledge of history and contexts (e.g. Graham style – traditional American contemporary dance – *Giselle* – romantic ballet – 19th century – Europe).

END OF KEY STAGE STATEMENTS (see page 175)
Statement c) is applicable to the above learning outcomes.

Detailed lesson content for the dance outcome

Dancing in the Rain in New Wellies   **Year 3   2 Lessons**

Dance framework

INTRODUCTION (approximately 16 bars of walking pace music)
Sitting on the floor – pull on to feet imaginary wellington boots. Admire them still sitting and/or standing up. Take weight on different parts of the feet – heels, toes, outside edges and look at them. Also lift up one foot at a time to look at parts of the boots – inside the boot, outside, bottom – heels and toes etc.

SECTION 1 (approximately 16 bars of skipping rhythm music)
Perform high knee movements – (skips, marches, gallops, hops, etc. with knees coming up high to 'show off' boots). Do these movements anywhere in the room.

SECTION 2 (approximately 32 bars of lively skipping rhythm music)
Perform running through, jumping into, kicking and splashing in puddles movements.

SECTION 3 (approximately 32 bars of lively travelling and leaping music)
   In pairs following the leader and performing in unison side by side perform a sequence of moves travelling and leaping over the puddles.

SECTION 4 (approximately 16 bars of walking rhythm music)
Walking, spinning, playing at taking weight on different parts of imaginary wellies to arrive back on the spot where the boots were 'put on'.

CONCLUSION (end of last phrase of music above)
Take off wellies and finish in a position looking at them.

Resources used during the lesson/s include appropriate music and the video snippet of Gene Kelly performing *Singing in the Rain* from the film.

Learning Activities

(**Bold** text below indicates the activity. Please see chapter 2 for ways in which this content implements the programme of study and end of key stage statements.)

1. **Exploration** task leading to identification of content for the INTRODUCTION of the dance
a) Introduction of the idea through **discussion** with children about the idea of having a new pair of wellington boots and playing in the rain should lead to free **improvisation** of movement to lively music. This would also make a good warm-up:

* expected range – running, jumping into puddles, splashing, stamping.

b) **Discussion** of the kinds of movements the children might use to **explore** examination and admiration of their boots sitting on the floor then standing.
Possible range of responses:

* sitting (turning toes up and down – both – one at a time); lifting up one leg and looking at all angles of it – sides, back, bottom of foot inside imaginary wellie; bending legs into frog-like position to see inside leg sides; and looking at one outside edge in a side sitting position and changing to look at the other by putting both legs on the other side, etc.

* standing (lifting one foot after the other forwards, backwards or sideways high); taking weight on different parts of the feet – lifting toes from ground and leaning forward to see and reverse with heels; looking at inside edges of feet, etc.

2. **Improvise** the introduction to the music.

3. **Performance** task for SECTION 1 of the dance: **practise** skipping, marching, hopping, galloping with high knee lifting movements (previously learned material) anywhere in the space, expressively 'showing off' wellies. Look for variety and energy, lift of legs and lightness. **Practise** SECTION 1 two or three times to music.

4. **Exploration** task leading to identification of content for SECTION 2 of the dance:

TASK – *perform running through, jumping into, kicking and splashing in puddles movement.*

Breakdown of task
a) Set imaginary situation – 'as in the warm-up, the floor is covered with puddles and you have your new wellington boots on – show me what you would do.'

b) Either through pupils demonstrating or through the teacher commenting with praise, take some ideas from observation of the children **improvising** in (a) and ask all the children to **practise** them – for example, running keeping the feet very close and almost skating over the ground; jumping onto two feet with an emphasis on making a big flat-footed splash; kicking with the inside edges of the feet; make stamping movements walking in a circle within the confines of a large puddle.

c) **View** the video of Gene Kelly's performance of *Singing in the Rain* solo dance and song. **Discuss** the kinds of movements seen and ask the pupils to keep one idea in mind for their own dance.

d) **Improvise** to the music for SECTION 2 of the dance.

5. **Creating** and **performing** improved for SECTION 2 of the dance through **viewing**

a) view the whole of the dance from the moment Kelly says good-bye to the lady.
Questions to encourage discussion:
• 'Why do you think he dances and sings in the rain?'
• 'How do you know he is happy?'
• 'Which movements do you remember best?'

b) 'View the part of the dance between the sung sections (nearly the whole of it!) and remember some of the movements which you really like – perhaps those which make you laugh.'
    Questions to encourage discussion:
• 'Which was your favourite movement and why have you chosen it?'
• With one of the children's choices in mind – 'Can we put some words on the board to describe it?' (For example – the flat-footed two to two feet jumps in the large puddle – words or phrases such as splat, splash, hit, smash, making frog-like jumps, large bounces as on a trampoline.)

- 'Is this the biggest splashing movement he performs?'
- 'Are there some other big movements you remember?'
- 'Are there any small or quiet movements?'

c) Improvise your dance in the puddles and try to use just one movement from the video.

6. **Perform** the dance from the beginning up to the end of SECTION 2. **Practise** all together, then **view** a few at a time. Question children about their peers' work and observe selected examples. Another **perfomance** all together might make a good ending for lesson 1. The next lesson could then begin with the dance so far as a warm-up and recall and **practise** activity.

7. **Create** a partner sequence of travelling and leaping for SECTION 3 of the dance
TASK – *with your partner create a sequence of running and leaping over imaginary puddles.*
a) **Practise** and **perform** running and leaping movements individually. The teacher should remind pupils of the different kinds of leaps they already have in their vocabulary – possibly by asking appropriate questions. The children should select and **practise** a range of leaps.

b) **Practise** two ways of **performing** with a partner. The teacher should set the task of children working in pairs following the leader – the follower copying the leader's run and leaping action in canon. The children should then **select** one kind of run and leap and **practise performing** it side by side in unison.

c) **Create** by combining the leading and following sequence taking turns, and the unison sequence. The following structure might help:
- A run and leap B follows copying – repeat with new leap
- B   "   "   "   A   "   "   –   "   "   "   "
- A and B run and leap together side by side with 2 different leaps.

8. **Practise** to improve skill and **perform** these sequences possibly extracting a few of the leaps and focusing the pupils' attention on the use of knees and feet in taking off and landing, i.e. taking off from the whole foot and 'pushing the floor away' and landing through the foot, toes first, into a soft bent knee position into travel. Also work on extension of legs and feet in the air (show Gene Kelly again perhaps), and uplifted back and head with arms used to gain height.

9. **View, discuss** and **appreciate** each other's **created** sequences and **performance** of them.

10. **View** the video dance again and note the movements used at the beginning and end of the dance, i.e. quieter and more pedestrian movements. **Appreciate** the bounce in Kelly's walks and try to get this feel in the children's **performance** of walking movements.

11. **Improvise** stepping actions taking weight on different parts of the feet – heels toes one flat one heel one flat foot knee bent one high on toes knee straight, outside and inside edges, etc., and spinning movements to **create** SECTION 4 of the dance.

12. **Create** own ending taking off imaginary wellies.

13. **Practise** and **perform** whole dance. The teacher could identify parts that need attention and provide the necessary teaching points using language, including the use of imagery, to improve the children's work.

14. **View** each other **performing** the whole dance. Look for expression (commenting on sensory and expressive qualities, e.g. bouncy happy walks, stretch flying leaps), continuity and phrasing (showing understanding of the overall form – beginning, middle and end of the dance). If possible video the children's **performance** to enable them to **view** themselves, improve and **perform** again.

15. **Appreciate** the dance experiences in the above two lessons through writing about the dances **created** by themselves and/or Kelly's dance. This work could also include painting a picture and writing a poem perhaps. Alternatively, if they have seen a video of themselves, the children could write an **interpretation** and **evaluation** of their work, even though the latter is not a required skill in this key stage.

Learning outcomes

By the end of two lessons children will have:

1. **Created** improvised responses for the INTRODUCTION, SECTIONS 1, 2, 4 and the CONCLUSION of the dance through exploration of appropriate movement content to symbolise the ideas.

2. **Created** a short sequence of travelling and leaping actions with a partner to show understanding of canon and unison and changes of relationship. The sequence should be memorised and repeated.

3. **Performed** and remembered the whole dance demonstrating understanding of the expression and form.

4. **Performed** and practised skills in order to improve technical and expressive aspects in them.

5. **Appreciated** the appropriateness and originality of Kelly's and their peers' movements in relation to the idea for the dances.

6. **Appreciated** and made comment on their own and others' created and performed dances.

7. **Appreciated** and used artistic and aesthetic language to describe and interpret the movements and dances.

Assessment in relation to end of key stage statements: (see page 157)

Statements a), b), c), e) and f) can be applied.

Detailed content of lessons for the dance outcome:

Pool Idling Year 9 3–4 lessons

Dance framework
Music: Introduction of *Shine On You Crazy Diamond* Pink Floyd (*Fame – A Collection of Great Dance Songs*)

INTRODUCTION (music – the first section prior to solo flute sound coming in)
    A few at a time at random enter slowly and dreamily from edges of the room to own spot – all facing one direction – move slowly into different positions – lying, sitting, kneeling, standing – stare dreamily into space watching imaginary people in the pool and perhaps doodling with hands or feet.

SECTION 1 (music – the first section up to the first solo guitar lead)
Stretch out into a lying position on backs, arms above heads. From this starting position create a solo sequence of motifs incorporating arching, curling, stretching, rocking and rolling movements giving an illusion of being in water, gently and slowly indulging in floating in it. Keep in contact with the floor most of the time but use one rising and falling action during the sequence.

SECTION 2 (music – the section up to the accented guitar lead)
Move to partner and perform motifs including assisted jumps, movements onto and sliding off partner, through, under and round partner, lifting and lowering partner. All of these movements should be performed in slow motion as if playing around in water.

TRANSITION (music – between the above section and the next prior to drum beats)
   At clapped-hands signal – all run as if through water to groups of four.

SECTION 3 (the section of music leading up to the words)
In the group of 4, choreograph a sequence in unison with one incidence of canon and employing at least one swimming action out of *Waterless Method of Swimming Instruction*. The sequence should be symbolic of receiving imaginary instructions from the side of the pool to improve swimming strokes.

CONCLUSION (the introductory music repeated)
Move into individual spaces – repeat and develop some of the solo sequence in section 1 and determine own conclusion.

Resources used during the lessons:

a) the music like the above mentioned by Pink Floyd without much beat or accent. It should be quiet and smooth like the music accompaniment for *Waterless Method of Swimming Instruction*.
b) the video recording of *Waterless Method of Swimming Instruction* (1980) by Robert Cohan.

Learning activities
(**Bold** text below indicates the activity. Please see chapter 3 for ways in which this content implements the programme of study and end of key stage statements).

1. **Exploration** tasks leading to **identification** of content for the dance:
a) Stretching, relaxing, arching, curling in and rolling movements in contact with the floor and standing up keeping the movement slow, fluid and continuous.

b) Extending upward movements into controlled falling actions sliding into the floor on different body parts.

c) Assisted jumping in pairs – using partner as object to push against without hold, e.g. step into jump from one foot at the same time pressing down on partner's shoulder or back. Partner acting as object assisting flight could be in different positions, e.g. kneeling on all fours for partner to jump off the back acting as a take-off platform but appropriateness for the context of partner work in water should be kept in mind.

d) Assisted jumping in pairs with aid from the partner supporting the jumper. Hands round the waist, under upper arm, clasped and receiving one foot, pushing hands against hands, pushing and lifting from behind between the scapuli during a jump – provide a few ideas. Students should find their own answers to this task but should keep in mind the theme of the dance when selecting from their explorations.

e) Movements onto and off partner showing a held moment with one person off the floor. Students should explore lifts, jumps into held positions and different ways of sliding or lowering to the ground to move out of held positions. Ideas might include – one partner jumping upwards to be caught by the other partner surrounding arms to hold close to him or herself clasping around waist or under buttocks and then allowing the held partner to slide down and touch the floor into a release fall. Alternatively, a partner might lift the other by taking his or her weight on one shoulder or on the back through the person to be lifted bending over and lying in contact with the body part to be used as a support for the lift. The lift occurs when in contact the lifter rises up causing the lifted person's feet to leave the floor. These are just two examples. There are many ways of achieving lifts and also many ways of moving out of the lift. Students might benefit from imagining the water environment to get the feeling of buoyancy and slow motion control.

f) **Exploration, abstraction** and **development** of motifs from known swimming strokes and exercises. Take aspects of breast stroke, crawl and butterfly for example and exaggerate, combine and add movements to them (jumps for example), make rhythmic phrases out of them, vary and develop them changing level and direction. These are just a few ideas. There are many ways in which motifs can be developed out of realistic action in order to become symbolic. Students should attempt to change the originating strokes as much as possible so that they create abstract symbolic actions which have distinctive rhythmic and stylistic features.

2. Compositions tasks leading to **selection** and **refinement** of content for motifs

a) Solo task for the introduction of the dance: 'Imagine a hot sunny day and being on holiday. You are going towards the swimming pool and you move slowly, savouring the thought of having a swim. You first of all just watch others in the pool though and enjoy the feel of the sun on your body. Select movements to travel from the side of the room into a space and choose a position to show that you are watching people in the pool.'

b) Solo task for section 1 of the dance: 'From the starting position lying on your backs with arms stretched along the floor and above heads, select movements from 1a) and 1b) above and link them into phrases to give the illusion of floating and moving gently in water.'
(32 bars of music)

c) Solo task for conclusion of the dance: 'Use some of the motifs you created for section 1, alter the order of them and develop them. This should finish with your own end to the dance (perhaps leaving the poolside or just lying out sunbathing).'
(16 bars of music)

d) Solo task for transition of the dance: 'Imagine travelling with large running actions across the pool and perform the movements exaggerating the use of legs and arms.'

e) Duo task for section 2 of the dance: select movements from exploration tasks 1c) 1d) 1e), link them together into **phrases/motifs**, then **refine** them, paying attention to the qualities of slow motion, fluidity and continuity to give the illusion of playing in water.
(48 bars of music)

f) Group of 4 task for section 3 of the dance: each student should contribute movement ideas from 1f) above to create a sequence of motifs to symbolise receiving swimming instruction from the poolside. The group should also select one movement idea from the video of *Waterless Method of Swimming Instruction*. Once the movements have been selected, the group should orchestrate them in space (varying the position of each dancer in the group) and in time (using unison and at least one incidence of canon).
(48 bars of music)

3. **Performing** tasks leading to **practice** and improvement of performance

a) **Perform** the introduction of the dance to improve expressive qualities and focus in order to symbolically portray the idea. Concentrate on achieving continuity, slowness and gentleness in movements to express tranquility.

b) **Perform** solo task for section 1 of the dance to partner, group or half class to demonstrate quality in composition and performance concentrating again on the qualities of slow motion, gentleness, and fluid continuity. Practise and improve qualities, phrasing, musicality and expressiveness.

c) **Perform** solo task for conclusion of the dance. This could be performed for a partner to start with so that the appropriate qualities are worked on to express the idea. The partner observing needs to be clear on what to look for, so it may be helpful for the pair to have devised and written a checklist prior to performing for one another.

d) **Perform** duo task for section 2 of the dance. This needs much practice to develop the technical skills appropriate for the actions and on several occasions during the exploration of content for this section, the teacher will need to break down the movement ideas into technical exercises towards improving performance. For example, the assisted jumps with one partner holding the other round the waist whilst jumping could be broken down as follows:

    i) practise jumping on your own two feet to two feet increasing size of jumps and swinging arms forwards and upwards to help elevation. Bend knees on landing and feel weight passing through the feet until both feet are fully in contact with the floor, heels down.

   ii) with a partner, practise three bounces and jump high pushing down onto partner's shoulders whilst partner who is lifting by holding round the waist pushes upwards at the height of the jump and bends with the jumper on landing.

  iii) repeat the above but without the jumper pushing down on partner's shoulders. The jumper can increase the height of the jump perhaps by extending arms from shoulder height up and reaching high during the jump.

   iv) repeat the above but travel into it.

    v) repeat but with lifter turning to change the direction of facingg for the landing.

   vi) repeat but with lifter letting go at the height of the jump and using different forms of jump, e.g. two feet to one.

In such a progressive way then, the students improve their technique in performance of assisted jumping skills gaining height, extension and control in landing.

e) **Perform** group motifs for section 3 of the dance to practise timing and group positioning.

f) **Practise** and **perform** parts of the dance combined and the whole dance to work on linking parts and expressive qualities. Performance skills such as extension, projection, focus, alignment and musicality should be observed, discussed and practised to improve the presentation of the dance.

4. **Viewing** tasks contributing to creating and performing tasks and **artistic and aesthetic appreciation** of the dance
a) **Viewing** of creative work in progress to make critical comment on appropriateness, originality and quality of own and others' work.

b) **Viewing** of the whole of *Waterless Method of Swimming Instruction* and parts of it in detail to gain ideas for their own compositions and to appreciate principles of abstraction into symbolism. The pupils might benefit from teacher-prepared worksheets which would guide their viewing of details in the choreography. They could then write about the dance noting the style of costumes, the historical context of the piece and the Graham style of Cohan's choreography.

c) **Viewing** of performance in performing tasks above to improve own and others performance of parts and of the whole dance.

Learning outcomes

By the end of three/four lessons students will have:

1. **created** solo motifs of dance content showing understanding of abstraction and elaboration of movement to symbolise meanings through appropriate choice of actions enriched with rhythmic, dynamic and spatial variation.

2. **created** a development of the motif/s in section 1 for the conclusion of the dance.

3. **created** partner motifs incorporating new skills of working in contact.

4. **created** group motifs employing previous knowledge of group orchestration of motifs and ideas picked up from the video resource.

5. **performed** and remembered parts of and the whole of the dance, demonstrating an understanding of the expressive meaning and form of it.

6. **performed** the dance showing understanding of performance skills such as projection, focus, group shape, body alignment, timing and musicality.

7. **performed** confidently and with technical accuracy the selected content of the dance, showing ability to co-ordinate, control, balance and extend, while performing combinations of actions coloured variously by dynamic and spatial patterning.

8. **appreciated** the appropriateness and originality of their own or others' compositions including the professional dance work, *Waterless Method of Swimming Instruction*.

9. **appreciated** and critically evaluated their own and others' performances and worked to improve them.

10. **appreciated** and critically interpreted the artistic/aesthetic aspects of choreography and performance in their own work, that of their peers and in Cohan's dance work.

11. **appreciated** the cultural historical context of Cohan's dance work.

Assessment in relation to end of key stage statements (see page 175). Statements a), b), c), and d) can be applied.

Alternative dance frameworks and learning activities from the programmes of study for dance key stages 1 to 3

DANCE FRAMEWORKS	LEARNING ACTIVITIES
1. *Balloon Dance* YEAR 1	*Programme of Study KS1*
Section 1: grow and shrink into different body shapes (balloon shapes) three times moving slowly, stopping and going to indicate blowing up	DANCE ACTIONS: whole actions – stretch and curl EXPRESSIVE FEATURES: Slow and interrupted
Section 2: float and burst with a jump to fall	DANCE ACTIONS: travel, jump and fall EXPRESSIVE FEATURES: soft, gentle travel and jumps free and up in space into strong quick jump and relaxed fall EXPRESSION IN DANCE: create image of balloons through the above and MAKING DANCES: create improvised responses to tasks; perform whole dance

Accompaniment: sound effect of blowing balloon up slowly three times. Light, soft continuous music for travel and bang on drum or children shouting BANG at the end.

2. *Journey on a Strange Planet*
YEAR 2

Programme of study KS1

Emphasis on use of feet:

Introduction: from sleep stillness get up as though sleep walking

Sections 1–4: use feet and knees on spot and travelling to suggest changing surfaces – bouncy (trampoline), sandy, sticky (treacle) and hot

Conclusion: spin into bed place and wake up from a dream!

DANCE ACTIONS: use of whole body – stretch into use of parts of feet – full variety

EXPRESSIVE FEATURES: quick, slow, light, continuous stopping in different directions

EXPRESSION IN DANCE: respond to changing stimuli with varied expression

MAKING DANCES: improvise within structured tasks; perform

Accompaniment: bouncy music (electronic perhaps) which also has changes in it for sandy and sticky parts. The hot section music could be played at double speed to achieve the effect in movement.

3. *Clown Dance* YEAR 4

Programme of study KS2

Section 1: travel with 'funny' runs – round 'ring' – variety

Section 2: create balances on different body parts – (funny)

Section 3: 'funny' walks taking weight of parts of feet – variety

Section 4: partner work – over under, through, around, on, off – create sequence

Section 5: repeat section 1 falling over to finish

DANCE ACTIONS: discover different runs and gestures, combine balancing/still body shapes;
discover different ways of walking.

EXPRESSIVE FEATURES: use combinations of speed force, continuity and aspects of space to vary

EXPRESSION IN DANCE: use music effectively; express 'funny' character appropriately

MAKING DANCES: improvise sections 1, 3 and 5; create motifs for 2 and 4; perform whole dance

Accompaniment: any lively circus music with a strong beat and clear phrasing.

4. *Storm Dance* YEAR 7
Whole class dance – solo in group

Section 1: from Karate position move across space with acceleration increasing size of steps; repeat 3 times end in space

Section 2: perform taught motif.

Section 3: rush to one side and perform 3 lightning actions; repeat to other side in unison

Section 4: rush to space and perform percussive solo storm

– thunder, lightning, rain, wind mixed to form repeated motifs

Section 5: rush in circle; jump with claps of parts touching in air, e.g. hands to knees; spin and fall to end

Programme of Study KS3

DANCE COMPOSITION: select from exploration to make martial arts motif into travel plus slow arm swirling;

select from exploration of striking actions using appropriate qualities – abstracting from forking, striking, sheet cracks and rumbles of thunder, pelting rain, etc.; improvise variety of percussive

ACCOMPANIMENT: use music phrasing and dynamic qualities to help dance expression

PERFORM SET DANCES: learn set motif; perform within the group

APPRECIATION: a range of viewing, describing and interpreting tasks in lessons including written work

Accompaniment: the above framework was created to fit Elgar's *Enigma Variations (Troyte)*.

5. *Group Togetherness*: YEAR 8

Task: In group of four create your own folk dance to symbolise group solidarity

Resources: Bruce's *Ghost Dances* Discussions about solidarity

Programme of Study KS3

DANCE COMPOSITION: use of Israeli steps and variety of formations plus canon

PERFORM SET DANCES: learn and perform two contrasting Israeli folk dances

ACCOMPANIMENT: use form in folk dance set music to create own dances

APPRECIATION: discuss ways in which each group distilled essence of style yet made the dance their own; record group formations/ patterns

Accompaniment: possibly part of *Ghost Dances* to ensure that it is not too close to pure folk dance. This should encourage students to make a folk/contemporary piece.

(This dance could be based on other styles such as African, S. Asian, etc. Teachers could use dance artists' input here.)

There are many ideas for lessons on composition and performance in my book *Dance Composition* (1992), which are suitable for KS4 and above. They include resource-based teaching/learning methods and should be most beneficial for students working towards GCSE.

6. The following description of ways in which a set technical study for GCSE or above could be used as a resource aims to help teachers deliver this seemingly teacher-centred and performance skill-oriented (*professional* model) aspect of dance education with a *midway* art of dance approach.

Appreciation of a technical study

Performing

1. Learn and perform a technical study set from a previous year's examination (GCSE/AS/A level)and available on video.

2. Description and analysis of content:
   a) describe and analyse the main actions in two contrasting sections of the study;
   b) notate or record them in some way;
   c) discuss with a partner whether or not the actions create the contrast;
   d) describe the qualities of the actions – speed, force, continuity and their role in making the contrast in the sections;
   e) notate and/or find words to describe the qualities using several words rather than one where possible;
   f) describe the use of levels, direction and size of movement to make the above sections contrasting.

3. Practise and perform the above two sections emphasising the contrast in actions, qualities and spatial features.

4. Video your performance and compare it with the professional example – analyse and evaluate:
   a) your accuracy in performance of actions;
   b) your ability to link actions into phrases with 'commas' and 'full stops';
   c) your ability to show qualitative contrasts;
   d) your use of space, e.g. clear changes of direction, overall coverage of the floor.

5. Describe and analyse the overall form of the study – motifs, phrases, sections, transitions, contrasts, climaxes and repetition of sections. Practise performing the study giving attention to these features of form.

6. Work in twos to identify key movements/short motifs which occur throughout the study.
   a) choose three of the above and identify:
   • exact repetitions;
   • developments of them and how they are developed;
   • number of times each is used.

b) identify the movements leading into and out of each of the repeats of the three key movements/motifs.

c) practise performing the movements/motifs making the differences clear.

7. Identify the style of the study:

a) list the features which create the style;

b) practise the sections of the study in which the features you listed are emphasised;

c) video your performance and evaluate the style of your movements;

d) practise to improve the style.

8. Describe the music, its type, its style, its expression and its form and discuss how these elements of music relate to the same elements of the dance:

a) listen to the music with your eyes closed and visualise the movements of the study;

b) select the section of the dance you find most difficult and listen several times to the music then dance it without the music but thinking the music in your head;

c) perform the section with the music (it should be improved if you have internalised the rhythm and phrasing).

9. Describe the study's use of space in the room:

a) draw the floor pattern of a section containing mostly travelling actions;

b) walk the pattern in the space ensuring that the full amount of space is used;

c) perform the movements using all the space;

d) dance the whole study concentrating on patterning in the stage space.

10. View the video performance of the professional dancer and analyse his/her performance skills – focus, alignment, line, projection to an audience, expression, light and shade, sense of form, use of music:

a) use this checklist to evaluate your own performance;

b) practise the aspects least good until they are improved.

The above study should help the student understand the extent of work that is involved in 'getting inside' a piece so that it is fully mastered. It is more likely that a successful performance will result if the student has thoroughly internalised the complexity of the choreography than if it is taught and learned by rote.

Choreography

1. Select the motif you like best in the study and use it as a basis for your own choreography:

a) as a solo:

- through development and variation of the content, actions, spatial features and through changing the qualities of time, force and continuity;
- using a different piece of music;
- giving it a different style.

b) as a duo or trio:

- through developing the content for one body and performing the original simultaneously with the development to make the relationship complementary;
- through orchestrating both the original and the development using canon and unison, changing spatial relationships and direction;
- taking the choreography further as determined by the group, possibly using different music and in a different style.

c) create a dance in the style of the technical study.

Choreography tasks based on a technical study from time to time will help students to become familiar with a vocabulary of movement which is new and different from their own. In most choreography situations, the source of content is dependent on the students' own limited repertoire. Employing a piece which students have learned for performance as a basis for choreography makes them use new movements or a new style in their own way. These then become a part of their repertoire.

Outline of content for an A level resource pack

A good resource pack permits flexibility of use in that it offers several routes through the content and different levels of learning. In the art of dance, the headings of choreography, performance and appreciation are a convenient way of organising the content.

Where to begin is the first decision to make in using a resource pack. If, for example, worksheets contain tasks which are progressive, the teacher could decide to introduce the topic of the resource pack by taking students through the first tasks only on each worksheet. Alternatively, students might benefit more if they were to undertake study of the appreciation section first. This should require them to put the topic into an historical and cultural context. Whatever is decided about the starting point, a good resource pack will promote developmental and progressive threads through each aspect of the topic, building towards an overall understanding.

Just as there are different routes through a resource pack there are many different ways in which to create a resource pack. The example below is just one way. There are many other ways of dealing with the same topic.

Example Resource Pack on Siobhan Davies

(It is important that this work is linked with at least one visit to see the Siobhan Davies Dance Company in live performance.)
a) Aims and objectives of the pack and possible routes through it identified.

b) Background information on Siobhan Davies from:
  The Dance Handbook – Robertson, A., and Hutera, D., Longman (1988)
  Striding Out – Jordan, S., Dance Books (1992)

c) Notes on some of Davies' works in chronological order. These are made up from a series of critics' or authors' statements and programme notes.

d) Essay or discussion questions based on the above readings.

e) Notes on *Bridge the Distance* 1984 – the background, structure, use of the group, music, design, costume and the dancers. Information is taken from an article by Mary Clarke in *The Dancing Times* (1985)

f) Appreciation: having viewed the video of *Bridge the Distance* students are required to consider:
• how the use of floor patterns and lighting might indicate the passage of time;
• how the development from duos to quartets might indicate a change of relationships;
• two lists of words – sensory and expressive – and underline at least four words in each column to describe the qualities in a particular solo.

g) Choreography: based on selected duo movements from the dance work. Students are required to:
• copy three actions where the dancers are in contact, e.g. balance, counter balance, lean, turn, lift;

- employ qualities listed above to link the actions into a motif;
- set the duo in spatial relationship with another duo;
- video the result;
- discuss how far it contains the essence of the Davies style.

h) Performance: learn and perform a solo style study (in the pack recorded in notation and on video). Work on improving performance through:
- considering the meaning and feeling in the words used to describe the movements in the voice-over on video – relax, drop, fluidly, sway, light, continuous, controlled, sustained, throwaway, smooth, sudden, lyrical, soft, giving;
- study of the video and the students' performances in some of the ways listed above for the technical study;
- write an essay on the features of the study which capture Davies' choreographic style.

The resource pack then leads the students through similar appreciating, creating and performing tasks based on *Wyoming* (1988) and includes much written material from journals, books, company packs, programme notes and video including an interview with Davies and pictures. It also includes listening to and study of the music and detailed analysis of the design elements. Comparative study of the two works helps the students to discern changes and developments in Davies' choreography. At the end of about half a term of work with the pack, the students will have developed in-depth knowledge about and appreciation of Davies, her choreographic style, her works and the Company. They will also have extended their own choreographic and performance abilities.

Bibliography
and Further Reading

Abbs, P. (ed) 1987 *Living Powers: the Arts in Education* Falmer Press

Abbs, P. 1988 *A is for Aesthetic: Essays on Creative and Aesthetic Education* Falmer Press

Abbs, P. (ed) 1989 *The Symbolic Order: a Contemporary Reader for the Arts Debate* Falmer Press

Arts Council 1993 *Dance in Schools* Arts Council of Great Britain

Best, D. 1985 *Feeling and Reason in the Arts* Allen & Unwin

Brinson, P. 1991 *Dance as Education* Falmer Press

Broudy, H. 1972 *Enlightened Cherishing* University of Illinois

Calouste Gulbenkian Foundation 1980 *Dance Education and Training in Britain* Calouste Gulbenkian

De Mille, A. 1960 *To a Young Dancer* Putnam

DES (DFE) 1992 *Physical Education in the National Curriculum* HMSO

Foster, R. 1976 *Knowing in my Bones* A & C Black

Foster, J. 1977 *The Influences of Rudolf Laban* Lepus Books

Gibson, R. 1982 'The Education of Feeling' in Abbs, P. (ed.) 1989 *The Symbolic Order: a Contemporary Reader for The Arts Debate* Falmer Press

Glasstone, R. 1986 'Selection and its influence on the training of dancers' in *The Growing Child in Competitive Sport* Hodder and Stoughton

Graham, M. 1935 quoted in *Martha Graham* Armitage M. (ed.) Dance Horizons, NY

Gough, M. 1993 *In Touch with Dance* Whitehorn Books

Harlow, M. and Rolfe, L. 1992 *Let's Dance: a Handbook for Teachers* BBC

Harrison, K. and Auty, J. 1991 *Dance Ideas for Teachers, Students and Children* Hodder and Stoughton

Harrison, K., Layton, J. and Morris, M. 1989 *Bright Ideas – Dance & Movement* Scholastic Publications Ltd.

Haynes, A. 1987 'Changing Perspectives in Dance Education' in Abbs, P. *Living Powers* Falmer Press

Jordan, S. 1992 *Striding Out* Dance Books

Laban, R. 1948 *Modern Educational Dance* Macdonald and Evans

Langer, S. 1953 *Feeling and Form* Routledge and Kegan Paul

National Curriculum Council 1992 *Physical Education – Non-Statutory Guidance* NCC
National Dance Teachers' Association 1993 *Dance Matters* Winter Term NDTA
Northern Examinations and Assessment Board 1993 *Dance* Syllabus for GCSE 1994
Osborne, H. 1970 *The Art of Appreciation* Oxford University Press
Pring, R. 1976 *Knowledge and Schooling* Open Books Publishing Ltd
Redfern, H.B. 1972 'Dance as Art, Dance as Education', in *Collected Conference Papers in Dance* (1973) A.T.C.D.E.
    1973 *Concepts in Modern Educational Dance* Henry Kimpton Publishers
    1986 *Questions in Aesthetic Education* Allen and Unwin
Reid, L.A. 1969 *Meaning in the Arts* Allen & Unwin
    1981 'Knowledge, Knowing and Becoming Educated' in *Journal of Curriculum Studies* vol. 13 no. 2
    1983 'Aesthetic Knowing' in Ross, M. *The Arts a Way of Knowing* Pergamon Press
    1986 *Ways of Understanding and Education* Heinemann Educational Books
Robertson, A. and Hutera, D. 1988 *The Dance Handbook* Longman
Russell, J. 1974 'Dance in Education – Artefact or Expression' in *Laban Art of Movement Guild Magazine* no. 52
Smith-Autard, J.M. 1992 *Dance Composition: a Practical Guide for Teachers second edition* A & C Black
Smith, J.M. 1976 *Dance Composition: a Practical Guide for Teachers* Lepus
    1982 'Technique and Style as aspects of Expression in Dance' in *Conference Papers in Dance* vol. 3 NATFHE and British Society of Aesthetics
    1987 New Directions in Dance Education in *The British Journal of Physical Education* vol. 18 no. 3
    1988 'Dance as Art Education: New Directions' in Young People Dancing 4th International Conference – *Dance and the Child International* vol. 1
    1990 'Dance Perspective on the National Curriculum' in *Towards the Future: Dance Education in the 90s* DaCi and NDTA
    1991 'Teaching Dance Performance in Secondary Education' in *The British Journal of Physical Education* vol. 22 no. 4
Spurgeon, D. 1991 *Dance Moves – from improvisation to dance* HBJ Publishers
Stevens, S. 1992 'Dance in the National Curriculum' in Armstrong, N. (ed.) *New Directions in Physical Education* vol. 2 Human Kinetics Books
University of London School Examinations Board 1992 *Dance* Advanced and Advanced Supplementary Syllabus
Ware, M. 1987 *Time to Dance* Belair Publications
Witkin, R. 1974 *The Intelligence of Feeling* Heinemann Educational Books

Dance works on video employed as resources in the text:

Cohan, R. 1988 *Waterless Method of Swimming Instruction*
Kelly, G. 1952 *Singing in the Rain* (MGM Film)

Glossary

Glossary of terms used in this book which are specific to education in England and Wales:

A level Advanced Level examination normally taken at the age of 18 or over.

AS level Advanced Supplementary post 16 examination which is worth half an A level.

GCSE General Certificate of Secondary Education normally taken by all secondary pupils at the age of 16+

National Curriculum The curriculum specified by the Government for all pupils aged 5–16 delivered during years 1–11.

Key stages progressive stages in the National Curriculum:
Key stage 1-years 1, 2 & 3 ages 5–7
Key stage 2-years 4, 5 & 6 ages 7–11
Key stage 3-years 7, 8 & 9 ages 11–14
Key stage 4-years 10 & 11 ages 14–16

End of key stage statements statements specifying the knowledge, skills and understanding which pupils are required to demonstrate at the end of each key stage through assessment at the ages of 7, 11, 14 and 16

Programmes of study (PoS) programmes which provide a basis for planning work to ensure that the prescribed knowledge, skill and understanding is gained in order that pupils achieve the attainment targets as defined by the end of key stage statements.
The PoS consists of three parts:
- general requirements which apply to all key stages – e.g. developing positive attitudes, solving problems

- general requirements for each key stage in order to achieve the objectives of the key stage

- subject specific requirements (the programme of study for DANCE within PHYSICAL EDUCATION is the focus of chapters 2, 3 and the Appendix of this book).

Index